A Gift to the Future *from* the Leisure Village *Writers*

Universal Wisdom
from Aroostook County Historians

Foreword by
Glenna Johnson Smith

Writing Facilitator
Martha Brabant Pritchard

BRIGHT STAR
PUBLISHING
CHAPMAN, MAINE

This book is dedicated to those who helped build
the history we endeavor to preserve for future generations.

Glenna Johnson Smith, teacher and friend,
who continues to inspire so many.

Phyllis Hutchins, who left our circle in October, 2015.
Though she didn't live to see our book's completion,
her stories play an important role in its content.
She is deeply missed.

Vaughn Smith

Commander John Holmes

Fred Burden

Roger Ouellette

Philip Chase

Dana H. Bishop

Arnie Davis

Vaughn Allen

Ross and Mabel Day

Jack and Eva Brabant

Henrietta Davis

CONTENTS

MEMORIES OF CHILDHOOD THROUGH TEEN YEARS

As We Became Adults

We Experienced Married Life

New Generations Join the March

WRITE IT DOWN
by Glenna Johnson Smith

I stare at a tintype of Great-Grandfather Proctor, a young man with curly dark hair and beard. His blue shirt is open nearly to his waist, and he is holding a pick ax. This stranger is a part of me. Some of his blood is warm in my veins. I have his hair, and probably other traits, good and not so good. I wish I knew more about him so I could pass on his truth to my sons and granddaughters.

If only he had jotted something down. I'd like to know what made him laugh and what scared him, what he ate for breakfast and why he left his wife and young son, never to return. A village story had it that he went to California to dig for gold, that his little bag of gold was stolen, that he was beaten up, and that an Indian woman nursed him. Later she bore him two sons, and still later, when the mother died the sons kicked him out. He wrote to his wife and asked for money so he could come home to Maine, but she didn't answer the letter. My mother, his only grandchild, didn't know whether this tale was fact or fiction, for nothing was written down. I wish I knew his side of the story.

Perhaps some day my great-great-granddaughter will find a picture of me and wonder who I was. I hope some of my scrawled and messy journals will have survived. I'd like her to know about my happy and my sad times. I'd like her to be able to pass me on in this parade that we all join for our time.

Just imagine if today all of us retired people in Aroostook County started writing down everything we remember: our favorite toys, our pets, our friends and school teachers, our parents and grandparents and the houses they lived in. One memory will remind us of another. What a block of social history we would amass! Think of the windows we'd open for our descendants.

In today's fractured and frantic world, it helps children to know who they came from. It doesn't matter how we write our history, as long as we do it. Three friends my age have written poems that tell their stories, several others have combined pictures and stories; even if we write for our families only, we may be surprised to find that our words touch others as well. Here's an example: my friend Gwen Haley Harman of Caribou compiled a book, *This I Remember*, for her nieces and nephews. She was sure it would not interest anyone else. The book is now in its third printing. (It is available at Pieces of Eight Bookstore in Presque Isle*) When I read the book I was so caught up by the humor, the insights, and the exact details of family life that I became a Haley and grew up on the farm with Gwen, her brothers and sisters, and Dolly, their pony.

I believe that we should keep on writing. If we don't tell our own truth, the Lord only knows what others will say about us after we're gone!

**This document is undated and was found by Rachel Burden in a pile of her precious memories. Glenna taught writing in a SAGE course in which Rachel was a participant. The bookstore referred to has been closed since around 2000.*

Preface

by Rachel Burden

Once upon a time, long long ago, I was in a prayer meeting in our church basement. The pastor, illustrating a point used "chain of memory." You know, where you suddenly say to yourself, "Now what made me ever think of that?" Then you're off, footing down the memory trail. "Oh I started with *that* and it just led to "*that 2,*" then I went on to *this-that*! I looked across the room at my grandmother. She was nodding, smiling, and looking so surprised.

"Oh, for goodness sake! Do other people do that too?"

Well, a new book in our library was like that for me. Its arrival was a bit weird. From a visit to Bates Dental, we acquired a magazine which described an essayist and his writings, *Speaking Frankly*, by Frank Connors. The book was for sale with proceeds to benefit "People Plus" an organization of seniors in Brunswick, Maine. Mr. Bates was very interested in learning about our writing group here at the Village.

"Why don't you keep the magazine?" So we ordered the book for our library. The author *gave* us the book and I was an eager first reader.

My eye caught the word "mayflower," so that was the first essay I read.

What a delight—a 90-year-old lady guarding the secret of her mayflower patch. (The ending will delight you.)

I began thinking, "I could write a similar tale. My father guarded his mayflower patch, until he became engaged, then he used it for a prenuptial stroll (with proper chaperones, of course.)

Then my "chain of thoughts" gave me a new story. What else was there for dating ideas for them?

Then my "chain of thoughts" wanted to know, how did she (my mother, Hazel) ever talk her very strict parents into letting her go to music school in Boston?

The chain goes on ... and so on!

Read—and your own story ideas will keep popping, I BETCHA!

Introduction
by Martha Brabant Pritchard

A Gift to the Future didn't start out that way. When the Leisure Village Writers began this project, it was as gifts to themselves. Writing is one of those unique experiences that work that way. It feels good. It feels right. And it brings indescribable benefits to the writer.

Two years ago I began meeting with this group as a way to work through my own writing. I needed an audience to get it right. They brought their work into the mix and a year ago I gathered all their stories, essays, and poetry into spiral-bound notebooks for them to share. After hours at my small office photocopier and two reams of paper, a volume was produced; a clumsy, unattractive hodge-podge of reproductions from hand-written to copies of copies of previously published pieces from regional publications. We all loved rereading each other's words.

Even then, it didn't yet strike me that we were holding in our hands a goldmine of history. When I agreed to teach a course in storytelling at the college for SAGE (Seniors Achieving Greater Education) one of the Leisure Village Writers came with me to share some of his work. Conversations began about the efforts of others at collecting historical writings in the community, and we had it! This is a gift! A two-way gift in that the writing and giving serve similar ends. We have all lived lives that held great lessons to us at the time—great enough to have formed indelible marks on our very persona. So often we say to our own kids, "wait until you grow up and face this, then you'll understand."

However, as one school administrator put it: "Society has changed so dramatically in the last two generations that we are losing the stories that made our community what it is today." We have become a country of wanderers. It is too easy to pack up a household and follow a good job sometimes across the continent. What we leave behind is our family and the history that has been building over time. Some stories remain—but all too often we don't get together enough to cement those stories in the collective memories of the generations that follow. We are, in fact, losing out as a society and as individuals.

In recording the words that I have been given, I worked diligently at preserving the English language as well as the actual stories. There is history to be found behind each comma, each unique phrasing, the use of parenthesis and other mechanics. I have changed very little.

Even if the writer is not a personal relative, just to wander the woods where he has been and to know what has been seen and done, makes the experience striking. My husband recently went wandering, with a Maine guide friend, and came upon the remnants of the logging tramway and railroad left to decay in the Allagash Wilderness. The experience was all the more meaningful because he'd read the accounts of our writers, Leonard Hutchins and William McConnell. Consider our other writers. After reading the tales of Rachel Burden and Marjorie Bishop, who of us will flush a toilet without a new appreciation of the miracle of plumbing? And when we get sick and someone snuggles us up and brings us a warm cup of soup, there will be Joan Allen's words to remind us of what love feels like.

Memories of
Our Childhood
through Teen Years

Any Port in a Storm
by Joyce Davis

I was born in New Jersey, because that's where my mother was. Her name was Ottobelle Worthen.

My father, Elmer Spencer, was interested in poultry and I think my mother wanted to get him away from Grandmother Spencer, who was a very domineering woman, so they left Vermont to develop a business in poultry in New Jersey. Traveling through southern New Jersey, Dad purchased eggs. He candled them to make sure of their quality, and sold them to the grocery stores. The Great Depression was not a good time to be in business and my father went through bankruptcy when the grocers couldn't pay their bills. The poor guy didn't stand a chance.

I was born in Maplewood, New Jersey on May 4, 1927 in the depth of a scarlet fever epidemic. My mother must have given me some immunity to the disease because I survived. She didn't. She died when I was four days old. My Grandmother Worthen traveled from Vermont to be on hand through my mother's confinement. She cared for me from the start. My mother breast-fed me for those first days before she died, probably saving my life. After that I sucked milk from a large spoon until bottles and nipples could be purchased. We were quarantined for thirty days because we were considered to be potential carriers of the disease. My brother Bob was two years older than I and, as soon as we were allowed to travel, my Grandmother returned with us to Bradford, Vermont. So it was that, for the first two years of my life, I was raised by my grandparents, Frank and Anna Lunny Worthen.

My Aunt Rona and Uncle Lou had no children and wanted to adopt us, but my father wouldn't give us up. I wish he had. Our lives would have been a lot different.

When I was two my father took us back to New Brunswick, New Jersey. He hired a woman to take care of us. I don't think she did a very good job; we were on our own quite a bit. Oh, here's a good story: Bob and I had figured out how to climb up a tall dresser by putting our feet on the knobs. One day we saw what we thought was candy on top of the dresser. We climbed up and took the bar of chocolate down. There was only one square missing and we ate the whole thing, arguing over the last bite. We didn't know it was really a laxative. We went out to play and soon we both realized we had a problem. The bathroom in that house was on the second floor and we raced up the steps. I recall sitting on the edge of the bathtub encouraging Bob to get off the flush—it was my turn!

My brother and I were very close and would have stayed that way if things had worked out differently. After a time I returned to my maternal grandparents and Bob went to live with my father's brother, Uncle Herrick Spencer in Addison, on the other side of Vermont. He was a dairy farmer, unmarried, with one hired man. There were no women in the house so, of course, I couldn't live there.

The Spencer family owned property on Lake Champlain. We had a spot we called "Button Bay" where we loved to play. During the dry season, when the water was low, the clay would dry around the cattails stems forming hard circles of clay. These circles came up with the stems as we pulled them and we called them button stones. It was always fun to collect our button stones!

When I came to live with Grammie Worthen, I grew up with my half-brother George Spencer, and we had some rollicking good times together. Our house was at the top of a steep hill and the school was at the bottom. When winter weather was just right, all the kids in our neighborhood went to school on sleds. George and I shared a sled. I rode on my belly with George lying on my back. He'd drag his feet to slow us down when I'd tell him to. That was quite a fast ride! When we got to the bottom of the hill we'd place our sled in the snow bank beside the road and head on to school. Mr. Hatch, the man who drove the milk truck, always picked up the neighborhood sleds and carried them up the hill for us on his truck, so we would be ready to fly to school the next day.

Back then it was different. When a child needed a home, somebody just took them in. It was "any port in a storm!" And life was filled with storms when I was a child.

In my junior and senior years of high school, George, Bob, and I went to live with Uncle Lou and Aunt Rona in Lebanon, New Hampshire. They had no children.

Now, here's a story I just love! We had a cat named Mittens. He was fond of taking his drinking water directly from the dripping faucet in the tub. The main part of the house—living room, dining room, kitchen and pantry—were on one side, with a long corridor connecting the bathroom, bedrooms, and the stairway to my attic room. My grandparents' room was right across the hall from the bathroom. One day my grandmother drew water for a bath and for some reason left the door open while she returned to the bedroom to retrieve a forgotten item. Mittens was thirsty and, as was his habit, he moseyed on down to the bathroom. We were sitting in the living room when we heard a loud splash. No one could figure out what the sound was until the soaking wet cat zoomed down the hallway. When he got to the middle of the living room floor he shook! Then he looked at us all accusingly and said, as only a cat can, *Why didn't you tell me?"* We couldn't help but laugh!

My husband Arnie had a similar childhood. His mother died when he was five years old. His brother Carl was a year younger. They both were sent to live in the Bangor Children's Home. Back then it was, really, "any port in a storm" for motherless children.

WHEN THE WATER CAME UPSTAIRS
by Rachel Burden

We're going to have a bathroom! What joyful news! Where do we start?

By using the closet space in Priscilla's bedroom and a hunk out of the upstairs hall, the carpenter and the plumber decided a small room could be squeezed in. A window would be needed; a half one over the tub was possible. The carpenter began his assignment, while the plumber moved outside for major problems battling July heat, flies, pipes, digging drains, and curious kids who were wandering about. The year was 1928; an upsurge in the economy made our dream seem possible.

Down the slope from our square house, was a small field, a farm road, a big orchard and then another house for the hired man's family. (Guessing distance, I'd say 5 minutes away for my 7-year-old legs.)

A cesspool spot was dug halfway, drainage ditches joined ditches across the driveway, and up to the cellar of the house. We already had running water from our well house, so the kitchen and the barn already had underground pipes. What seemed like an impossible scenario to us was just another job to Allen Plumbing Co. People all over the area were adding bathrooms.

A sharp memory for my sister Mariam was the time she locked the bathroom door and couldn't undo the trouble. Her wails brought rescuers from all directions. One brother went out a bedroom window to the piazza roof to try to add comfort through the new bathroom non-open type window, while another brother was unscrewing hinges on the new bathroom door. The five-year-old was saved and cuddled. No need for a scolding!

She was so young and trouble seemed to beg her attention. Checking a container used by the plumbers, she found a hot adhesive for joining pipes, tested it with a finger and decided it wasn't pudding after all!

Saying good-bye to the outhouse was very gratifying of course, but nothing could ever compare to the excitement of that first tub bath. We were used to Saturday night ablutions in the galvanized zinc washtub. Often you were second or third in water saved from another sibling. In cold weather the drama took place in front of our black wood stove with the oven door open.

My brother Merle shared a funny tale: Once when he was in the tub and someone knocked at the kitchen door, step-mother Hazel grabbed the tub's side handles and pulled tub and Merle to the privacy of our separator-room. "Not funny," Merle reported. "I still remember how fast we went. It bruised my rear-end."

In good weather, Dad and the boys took soap and towels to the stream down back for the weekly bath.

The new bathroom was such a joy for the whole Higgins clan, but none more so than Grammy. She kept saying, "Imagine that I lived long enough to enjoy such a miracle!"

My First Train Ride
By William McConnell

In 1923 when I was seven, in early winter I became sick with what eventually developed into pneumonia. My mother, concerned that I was likely getting worse, sent a man some twenty miles into the woods to where my father was in charge of a small lumbering operation to urge him to come home.

My father bundled me up and we boarded the train at Portage headed south. We got off at Squa Pan Junction to change to the train for Presque Isle.

Shortly before, the railroad snowplow had accidently hit the end of the station platform, moving the whole building enough to ruin the chimney beyond use, leaving the waiting room as cold as the outside. The wait of an hour or more in the unheated station with a very sick child must have been an added worry to my father.

Once aboard the train, and fortified by a few sips from the trainman's thermos, we made it to Presque Isle Hospital where, that night, I had the first operation for drainage that set me on the road to recovery, though I was there most of the winter and was held back a year at school.

My Favorite Things
by Joan S. Allen

My growing up years were cousin-filled. They were more my age than some of my other friends and to be with them was fun for another reason—I was an only child and they had brothers and sisters. There was always something going on and I was always asked to stay for a meal and adults at the table always talked to everyone. At home our meals were pretty quiet.

The cousins always had something they might say—like questions to the elders, "M-I-K?"

I never questioned them about it but it finally came to me that they were asking, "More In Kitchen?" They didn't always agree with each other about things they wanted to do. The boys almost always argued with each other, sometimes coming to blows. I knew that they loved each other but it was different than my home where it was quiet as long as I practiced piano every day and got to school on time.

"Nanny," Della Hoyt Stevens, provided a warm home to that family for some time during growing years. Nanny lived just below the Training School and had a flower shop there—the Hardy Garden Co. She had a small shop attached to the house and sold pottery which I thought was lovely. She kept her ribbons and such in a small cupboard there. I had that cupboard for years and wish I still had it. I kept it for boots, mittens, and caps and gloves. It was very handy for me and for our family.

Nanny had a "Tea Room" in her garden for a few years and hired college girls to wait on guests. She outlived her husband, David Stevens, by many years. She lived to be over ninety years old.

MEMORIES OF DAD
by William McConnell

It started when she gave him a choice
   To get breakfast or dress the kids.
When we were able to dress ourselves
   He still made breakfast anyway.
I'd come down to hear him threatening
   That he'd apply the hot pancake turner
To an obvious portion of her anatomy
   If she didn't get up and get dressed.

Years spent guiding in the back-country
   Had turned him into a good cook.
Complimented on some dish, he'd say
   "I must have made a mistake."
Once he made a cornbread
   And left out part of the leavening.
He said, as he served the sorry thing,
   "I must have done everything right."

In the late 20s he'd be gone a month,
   Guiding hunters for V.E. Lynch,
At the Forks, Spectacle, and the Owl's Roost.
   One day he'd come in the door,
With his rifle and big leather pack,
   Bewhiskered, smelling of tobacco and sweat.
A kiss for Mother, while clasped to each leg,
   The littlest children welcomed him home.

WHERE I LEARNED TO COOK: MY MOTHER'S KITCHEN
by Phyllis Schwartz Hutchins

My mother, Merinda Russell Schwartz, ran my first kitchen and my first cooking classroom. That kitchen was on the one end of the house, but it was the center of our lives.

From the kitchen, four doors gave passage to a front porch, a back woodshed, upstairs, and to the sitting room and the rest of the house downstairs. Two large windows over a couch and a smaller one over a huge, black sink, opened onto the front porch. A cream separator sat beside the sitting room door, and an arm-long, battery-powered radio with hand-sized knobs sat on a sturdy shelf near the separator. A hand-operated, up and down butter churn sat beside the front porch door.

There were walls of cupboards and a gigantic black-iron stove with a large woodbox beside it and an earthenware wine crock behind it. Two large chairs and two very long benches were matching furniture for a porch sized table. I saw Mother's kitchen as a child, so perhaps it wasn't quite as large as I remember it.

Breadmaking—My earliest memory is of Mother making bread in the kitchen. My younger sister and brothers played around us as I stood with her at our big, plain, wood, kitchen table. Her breadboard, perhaps three feet square, rested on a corner of the table. The board had a rounded front edge and a low wood railing around three sides to keep flour and other ingredients corralled.

My head propped up in my hands, I leaned on the table and watched the fascinating process. Mother's shoulders, arms, and fingers moved rhythmically as she kneaded flour into a quite-round dough ball. She flattened the ball folded and patted the flat back into a quite-round ball again, and again pressed it flat. Suddenly she folded the dough over the edge of the breadboard and onto the floor. She quickly bent over, scooped up the soft, flat mass, flopped it back onto the breadboard and continued kneading with no loss of motion. She glanced at me quickly. "Don't you tell anyone that I dropped that," she said.

Many years passed before I told of that incident. At about the time of the bread-making incident, mother began to let me cook, make mistakes, try again, and learn. I also learned that much of our lives were spent to supply Mother's kitchen.

Father, my older brothers, and neighbors cut ice in early spring on the Aroostook River and packed it in sawdust in the woodshed to be used for refrigeration and making ice cream. Father and we older children picked berries and hazelnuts along field rows and in cut-over woodlands. We didn't come home until our pails were full.

Game shot in the summer was used quickly so it wouldn't spoil and also so the game warden wouldn't find it. We planted, weeded, hoed, protected from animals, and harvested a huge garden. Part of the grain crop was traded to the miller in Aroostook Junction, New Brunswick for grinding another part into flour. Part of the potato crop was sold in Fort Fairfield to purchase groceries. We older children milked the cows and brought the milk to the kitchen to drink, for cooking, and to be separated into cream.

Artist and Superwoman—In her kitchen, Mother was both artist and Superwoman. Regulating and cooking on a wood-burning stove, making butter, preserving all sorts of food, sewing clothes, and raising eight children were arts. Carrying water from a well in the yard and wood from the woodshed when father was away and we children were at school; washing clothes on a washboard; feeding her family, many visitors, and harvest crews; and having us children in the room near the kitchen were jobs for Superwoman.

However, even Superwoman gets tired. Perhaps many long nights remaking clothes by kerosene lamp light with the treadle-operated sewing machine contributed to her fatigue. One evening two hobos came to our kitchen door looking for a meal.

Hobos were not tramps. During the Great Depression they were good men for whom there were no jobs. They moved continually, doing whatever they could find for meals. Since the Canadian Pacific Railroad tracks ran through our yard and Mother was a kind, generous person many hobos stopped by. That night Mother was just too tired to feed them. She worried and fretted for two days, until she found that a neighbor had fed them.

St. Merinda—In 1939, Mother left our family farm, which had been home to all of us. Hard work and fatigue did not influence her decision. My oldest brother, Herbert Junior, a boy who worked like a man to help support the family, a boy Mother allowed precious radio time to listen to his favorite Wheeling, West Virginia Saturday night program, died of appendicitis because he did not receive medical help soon enough. Mother moved us from the hard-earned cornucopia of our farm to Fort Fairfield and the uncertainty of life without income during the Great Depression. There, we seven remaining children would be near medical help.

My mother, artist and Superwoman, might also have been St. Merinda.

No TV: Whatever Did You Do?
by Rachel Burden

"Hurry with the dishes. Most of the neighbors are here already. What do you suppose they'll want to play tonight? Maybe *Keep Away or Dodgeball?*"

"Let's teach them that new one the boys made up—the one with the sticks. I'm sure we'll have enough players for two teams. Remember how we try to steal sticks and not get caught? Or if caught, you stay in prison until rescued. What fun it is!"

Farm kids were the luckiest people in the world. Next to having a barn, having large, unmowed lawn was another big plus. Our game menu stretched from *Kick the Can, Cowboys and Indians, Scrub Baseball, Hailey Over, and more.*

Later, *Badminton* and *Volleyball* were added to the list.

"Dad, have you seen Mr. Beckwith's new lawnmower? You push it, and a cylinder goes around and mows the grass. Why don't you have one?"

"I already have lawnmowers. They're on the lawn right now—in the volleyball game."

Our Living Room
by Joan S. Allen

I had a great dad. He could do many things for and with me as I grew up. He worked as a bookkeeper in town and liked meeting customers. His mother, Annie Black (from Searsport) died at 35 and father (David) married again, this time to Della Hoyt from Easton.

I loved "Nanny" (Della) and she was to have three children of her own. So Dad had two half-brothers and a sister. Ruth, the sister, grew up and married a local boy and *their* children and I were "cousins" (though maybe they were half-cousins). Dad learned much from Nanny. She was a gardener and became a florist and Dad was always planting something—rosebushes, vegetables, raspberry bushes, and small trees. For a while we had a line of elm trees but they had to be taken down because of disease. Then he planted some oak trees. I might have been six or seven at the time. The oak trees have survived to this day and are way above the house! Dad and "Aunt Ruth" remained good friends their whole lives.

In our house, in the living room, there was a fireplace with two cupboards on each side. Mom's cupboard was where she kept her patterns (boring), but she did teach me how to sew. But in Dad's cupboard on the other side, I could open it and find all kinds of fun stuff. He not only used it for matches to start fires, but it had old cameras in it and old newspaper articles and an old mouth organ, with four scales on it which I taught myself to play and other stuff. I suppose when he married he took all his stuff with him when he left Nanny's house and had one of his own.

There was an old banjo in the attic with only one string left on it (I wish I had it now). There was a bookcase underneath the cupboard and I could climb up to the cupboard. I spent many happy hours there. Mom bought a set of Compton's Encyclopedia and I loved the animal stories in those as soon as I could read. Dad had a row of Zane Gray books and I read all those too.

That living room was where I stayed during measles, chicken pox, etc., because they would drag the sofa near the warm fire and put me, my pillow, and like as not, my cat, on the sofa. Mom would keep the fire up all day and bring me meals. I loved my soups. I didn't mind if I missed school, it was so comforting there. On the sofa in front of the fireplace!

At night Dad and I listened to the radio together, while my mother did the dishes. I loved it all even though I had to wear glasses and my mother made my clothes.

THE SCHOOL TEAM
by Rachel Burden

"Come on sleepy heads, the crust is perfect, I will have time to slide a while before the school team gets here."

What a wonderful way to be awakened by your mother on a crisp March morning!

We crossed the road to the neighbor's rock pile and exulted in the frosty air and the joy of going sliding with Mama as we sped down the hill again and again. Suddenly my brother called out the warning that the school team was coming. We dashed across the road, changed to school clothes, grabbed our lard pail lunches and were at the mailbox eager for our ride to school. We might not have been quite so eager had we known of the adventure awaiting us on the other side of our hill.

The school team was a double sled with a shacky house built on its top. Inside, the floor was covered with straw and up front was a small wood stove. Benches lined each side. Mr. Gregg, our driver, scared me half to death. He had a gray grizzled beard, chewed and spat tobacco juice and loved to pinch the girls, especially the smaller ones. Even if it meant being a bit cold, I always looked for a seat near the back. I loved to stare at the High School girls. They looked so glamorous with their short wavy hairdos. They held textbooks with composition paper inside showing from top to bottom. I decided that when I was 16 or 17, I wanted to look just like them. Their names sounded so musical that I loved to say them over to myself at night. There was Necia and Lila, Doris, Avis and Glennis, Thelma, Glenna and Flora, and yes even a Rachel! I liked that.

The wooden plows with their wide wings and the wooden rollers had kept the road well groomed all winter, but now that it was spring, the traveling became a bit skittish. On the other side of the hill from home, we felt that the big sled was swaying sideways. From the look on Mr. Gregg's face and the way he talked to the horses, we knew he was very concerned. Halfway down the hill, was a fairly level area and for a moment the horses seemed reassured. Then we started to traverse the lower hill and the sled began a horizontal slide. Mr. Gregg deftly maneuvered the reins talking calmly to the horses, while he drove the team out into a snow-covered, hilly potato field, ending up in a neighbor's dooryard and then back to the road. We were a scared bunch of passengers, but so grateful for the skill of our teamster. My fear of the old man seemed to diminish from that morning and I survived pinches and nose tweaks from then on, trying to act casual and friendly.

Maple Grove School
by Donna Dolly Cyr Pelletier

My life began in Maple Grove. I was born in the house I was brought up in, until the age of eight. My grandparents were Robert and Ina (Kennedy) Plummer. My grandmother gave birth to Robert Plummer, Jr. on May 5, 1931 and I was born on June 5, 1931. We passed for twins, until we were teenagers.

Memories from Maple Grove School days will always hold a special place in my heart. I remember the winters, especially in the late 1930's. We were picked up with a school team, which consisted of two horses pulling a large enclosed house-shaped sled, heated by a woodstove and driven by Warren Sawyer. During the spring and fall months, Stephen Ames picked us up with horses pulling a wagon.

On the first day of school in 1935, Bob, Jr. sat with me as I waited to be picked up. He decided he didn't want to go to school that year, so I was always a year ahead of him. That first day I had a brand-new cotton dress with cotton panties to match. I went down the slide at recess, tore both the dress and the panties, and was sent home for the rest of the day.

Maple Grove School had two rooms, one was for grades 1st through 4th, the other held 5th through 8th. Marilyn Hoyt Chase and I became lifelong friends. Our teachers were Clara Webb, and Mr. John Abernathy, who boarded with Tom and Zenith Houghton. No matter what class he was teaching, we had to pay close attention. Marilyn and I were chosen almost every day at lunchtime, to walk up the hill to the Houghton home and carefully carry Mr. Abernathy's lunch back to the school. Sometimes we would spill some, and every so often we would bravely sample the goodies. We must have done a good job though, for he never complained. I remember each day at recess time—snow, rain, or shine—we went out on the school porch and inhaled six deep breaths of fresh air.

On our "Graduation Day" from 8th grade (1948) we went into town to the Jenkins School, where we were arranged according to our height. Lawson Fisher and I were the tallest. Therefore, we proudly marched last in line to the Paramount Theatre, where the ceremony was held.

We learned so much from our Maple Grove School days. Every time I drive by that location where the building once stood, I have such warm and wonderful feelings of having once been a part of that special school.

Irwin's Dolls
by Rachel Burden

This story is half memory and half old tales from the older brothers. When my brother Irwin was little, his security blanket was a ragdoll named Dinah. It was made by Great-Grandmother Mazie McGlauflin (Grammy Mac). Apparently Dinah died when I was very small because I don't remember her. They say that Irwin carried her everywhere inside and out. One day she was dropped in the space where we had the garden and left there. Irwin hunted for her but in the meantime Dad plowed the garden and Dinah was gone forever. His great anguish was not appreciated by the older brothers who teased him most cruelly.

Now Peter I do remember! Grammy Mac went to her rag bag again and fashioned a most elegant male doll. He was stuffed, but was mainly flat overall. His clothing was non-removable but was so stylish, complete with fancy pants, coat and tie. His embroidered face had a charming smile and Irwin loved him. At the same time, dolls were given to Mariam and me, but I don't remember much about them. (Store dolls were still a future experience.) Peter seemed to be the favorite of all of us. One New Year's Eve, Mama stayed up late to make a special surprise for all of us. The dolls had become soiled with age and usage, so Mama took from her rag bag pieces and revamped the clothing and the faces. Instead of the great joy and appreciation that she expected from us, there was a great silence. Who were these newcomers before us? Unfamiliar faces and the new decor had turned these clumps of rags into strangers. We tried to say thank you, but the old companions were gone and part of our childhood had forever disappeared. Irwin had finally outgrown the doll era.

Early Sledding
by William McConnell

My first sled was a child-sized model of a typical one-horse-drawn sled, carefully and impressively made by the blacksmith/woodworker at a lumber camp where my father was in charge. I used it several winters; left by the side of the road in front of the house it was eventually stolen. The Flexible Flyer type of sled was just coming along, a style we disliked because it dug into packed snow on our hill. The preferred sled had low wooden sides shod with runners of round steel rod. One rode on one's stomach and steered by dragging the feet, hard on the toes of our boots but effective. This was before the roads were kept clear of snow; so that, after winter had really set in, no autos were to be seen 'til spring. A hill packed for sledding would stay in condition for weeks with no danger from autos. Memorable were clear, cold evenings, with clouds scudding across a full moon. Walking up the hill and sliding down, over and over, one had the feeling that the night could go on forever. Home at last to find, when boots were pulled off, that they were coated inside with frost.

Someone in town had made an elaborate, long bobsled. Usually once during the winter, when conditions were right, a horse towed the bobsled to the top of the hill leading north out of town, and six or eight young adults climbed aboard for one run.

Sawmill Town
by William McConnell

When I was quite young, the life-blood of the town was the sawmill, operated by the Portage Lake Mill Company.

The railroad came out of the woods from the south, looped around the end of the lake, and went back into the woods, headed north to Fish River or Fort Kent. At the village end of the lake, virtually everything between the railroad and the lake was related somehow to the mill. There was the mill itself, situated close to the water, with spur tracks leading into the rear, where the finished lumber came out, ready to be piled if not on immediate order, or loaded into railcars.

The mill ran on steam, generated by burning sawdust and shavings. There was a burner, a tall brick chimney to burn off scraps of no value. The single-cylinder steam engine was impressive, with flywheel nearly two stories tall. To watch the Pitman Arm flick by every second, transferring the back-and-forth motion of the piston to a rotary motion to turn the flywheel, all this in almost complete silence, was awesome as seen by a child. By means of shafts and belts, all the mechanical working of the mill was powered by this engine.

Spruce and cedar logs were cut each winter on the Fish Lake watershed, landed on the bank of the river or on the ice of the lake. Farmers could sell the oats and hay they raised to lumbermen, and work their teams of horses in the woods in winter, getting out the logs.

Many winters, from WWI through the early twenties, my father took charge of one of the small operations along the river, but the greater part of the yearly cut needed to keep the mill running was made by the mill company itself, up the valleys of the streams feeding Fish Lake. The year's cut was gathered in a boom when the ice went out in the spring. By a capstan and anchor arrangement the boom was towed the length of the lake to the outlet, and driven down the river to Portage Lake, where the logs were again formed into three or four booms for storage. A piledriver drove a cluster of three spruce logs into the lake bed to act as a tie-up for the booms.

Through the summer, a steam donkey engine mounted on a scow tethered just off-shore, pulled all the logs out of the water and piled them on land. Long ago it had been learned that frozen logs do not saw properly; the answer was a "hot pond" formed of tongue-and-groove plank driven into the lake bed, and kept from freezing by steam piped into the water. All winter long logs were pulled from the storage pile into the hot pond, which took the frost out of them, and were fed into the mill for sawing.

Big, straight cedar were sent to a pole yard to be peeled for utility poles. The rest of the cedar cut was fed into a bank of shingle machines.

A wakeup whistle sounded at five o'clock, followed by a six o'clock whistle to start the work day. The mill hummed with the whine of the saws, the piledriver might be working, the donkey engine puffing away at log piling. With two passenger trains and two freight trains daily; in summer especially, there was a sense of great activity.

Events Remembered
by Leonard Hutchins

My birthday was March 23, 1930. A touch of dementia notwithstanding, I remember a 1934 snowstorm. Perhaps I remember the snowstorm because my parents referred to it for years afterward.

Dad had a hernia. Mom shoveled a path from our front steps to Brunswick Street in Fort Fairfield. I could not see over the snow path walls.

A town shoveling crew cleared Fort Fairfield streets, first from the road center, then wide enough for traffic. Men standing on the snow piles looked like they were on house roofs. Snowplows then just couldn't handle it. Mom made a lot of coffee. Someone delivered our groceries.

Directly across Brunswick Street from our house was the Fort Fairfield Hacker School. Each schoolroom for grades one through four appeared potato-field big. A central assembly area added another half-acre, in my memory. Thick brick walls and window ledges all around made our Hacker School humongous huge in my opinion. As far as I knew it came with the world.

Johnny, a neighborhood kid, claimed he could climb anything. I think he could. Using window ledges, brick cracks, and the eaves, Johnny climbed the flat-roofed Hacker School. He bragged to me that he had actually seen the neighborhood nighthawks' nest.

I had to see that. A family of nighthawks had always nested on the Hacker School roof. I waited until Mom and Dad were away, dragged the family ladder to the Hacker School, and climbed to the roof. Sure enough! There in a corner was the shaggy nest, and the nearly-black birds. They lifted their wings and hissed at me. I am proud of myself. At about age twelve I had sense enough to leave the birds alone.

I couldn't decide if graduating from fourth grade at the convenient neighborhood Hacker School to the mile away fifth grade at Fort Fairfield Grammar School was a good deal. Walking a mile to school was a bummer, but dad bought me a bicycle. Wow! Super. But leave it to me to louse up a good deal. I soon learned to bicycle-jump sidewalks and be a dangerous nuisance in traffic. I almost caused an accident one day. I wasn't smart enough to run before the lady driver caught me. I heard things I didn't hear at home.

Some events don't seem all that important when they happen. For instance, one of my school friends caught a trout. Out of curiosity I asked questions. Surprise. Surprise. Mom knew more about fishing than anyone else. How could that be? Women, you know, don't know anything about outdoors—well, except doing the flower garden maybe. Mom told me that her father, my grandfather, was a logging crew foreman. Mom had spent her "being a kid" years in the woods. I asked mom about fishing, and I got more answers than I asked questions.

Fishing rods, casting, bait, hooks, maps, compass (Learn that!) I heard it all. Checking my map, I rode my bicycle to a far-away swamp. Following map and compass I found the brook. The fishing was great. I walked back with my compass in my pocket. Eventually I dug my compass out and found my way home by moonlight. Mom was glad to have me home, but she was not very proud of her little boy.

I had no idea the next event was coming. I parked my bicycle in the garage and trotted into the house as usual. Whoa! Wow. Mom and Dad had chairs pulled to the front of the radio. They were listening. Intently. Dad raised his hand to keep me from interrupting the man speaking on the radio. Mom sat, her elbows on her knees and her head resting in her hands. Mom was crying.

The man stopped talking on the radio. Dad lowered his hand. I asked, "What happened?"

"That was President Roosevelt talking," Dad said. "We are at war."

"Again," Mom said.

Mom hung a small one-white-star flag in our front window. She explained that the flag represented my brother, Gardiner, who had joined the U.S. Navy. She told me of friends she had lost in World War I. She cried. I felt older. Much older.

When I walked to school that winter, there were far fewer young men on the street. They were in the armed services. Young women had moved to be near war material factories. I didn't have to wonder long if a kid like me could help somewhere. Every weekend either Dad took me to a friend's farm or the farmer came after me to work in his potato storage barn for the weekend. What a deal! We got paid and we soon learned that our teachers didn't push us to do homework. However, packing tons of potatoes was hard on the back.

My dad, too old for any of the armed services, became an air raid warden. During an air raid drill I followed Dad as he checked house after house to see that no curtain was loose and no light escaped. I felt like a peeping Tom.

That was a little silly—maybe. Our enemies' airplanes didn't have fuel capacity enough to reach us and return home. However, we didn't know if our enemies were building better aircraft. Fort Fairfield also installed huge air raid sirens. Those things were gut-twisting scary—ominous, for sure.

Wars end. Sirens unwind. People change. When I entered high school I felt that I had grown up and learned enough already. I wish that were the last mistake I've made since.

The "Tappers"
by Joan Allen

I can't remember which year it was that a class in tap dancing was given in downtown Presque Isle in a small building on State Street across from Olore's Law Office. Me and Nan, Christine, Sis and others (there were about ten of us) thought it would be fun to go there and take the class once a week on Saturday. As I remember it cost 50 cents each time. We were to have black shorts and loose white blouse and taps on our shoes.

I guess that our parents didn't object to the initial expense because we all showed up on the right day with the right clothes and our money and began to learn the rudimentary step I've never forgotten— "DOWN—one-two-three—DOWN"—which could be used on either foot. It was fun when we could do it together just like in the movies. Maybe the class lasted a month or two, but it was fun! Although none of us had further careers in this dance, it was probably a good lesson as to how to DANCE once we were in high school and introduced to ballroom dancing—although no one asked us to tap then!

It's all Right to Write
by Rachel Burden

How do I describe my passion for writing without sounding like a braggart? Instead let's call it history and let readers decide.

Because I was a little older than my first grade friends, I found things easy and boring. Miss Blackstone decided that I really should try second grade.

"No," said Hazel, my mother. The next time Hazel was in town she bought a large yellow tablet and a couple of penny pencils.

"Now," said Hazel to Rachel, "the next time you have nothing to do, WRITE."

That was a beginning.

At home one of the desk drawers was filled with old business letters recycled so that we kids could write or draw. Early ventures included Mariam writing a poem which was sent to our Sunday School paper and was published. Later I entered a contest sponsored by the WCTU [Women's Christian Temperance Union] wrote an essay, won first prize—a dollar! I bought my first Bible.

School was fun through the years, especially when tests were essay tests. While teaching in Calais, I had an article about encouraging children to write published in *The Maine Teacher*. In Presque Isle while at Training School, an article of mine was published in *Early Years*, a national teacher's journal. This one I titled "Dear Jonathan, Maybe Tomorrow." Jonathan needed more than tomorrows. He had trouble with 4+3 but could tell me how many moons it would take to cover the sun.

LIBBY BROOK
by Leonard Hutchins

My mom had a knack for choosing the absolute best toys for me. In about 1938 (my birthday was March 23, 1930) Mom introduced me to my first outdoor world—Libby Brook—a super toy.

Libby Brook was, depending on the time of year, about ten feet wide, knee deep, and colder than it needed to be. It ran across under Main Street, Fort Fairfield near my dad's garage. A restaurant is there now. My friends and I could always catch enough trout to impress the old folks, my mom in particular. It was a good world.

However, during spring ice-out and high water, the Aroostook River sometimes invaded too much of Main Street. The town built a dike to keep the river where it belonged, and Libby Brook was changed to flow around the town.

Libby Brook had been my world, and my world had changed. But, well, it was still Libby Brook and my world—sort of.

Just out of curiosities sake, one day I wandered up what used to be Libby Brook. I found where the brook had been changed to flow around the town. Hey! Guess what? Libby Brook flowed through acres and acres of bushes and trees now. And there, all over the soft, muddy places, was the backwoods newspaper. Tracks. Everywhere: deer, raccoon, fox, rabbit, somebody's dog, partridge, little sparrow-sized birds—and a bird track as big as my hand. It had to be an eagle.

When I returned home from that trip up the brook, I told Mom about the eagle tracks I saw—three or four times as big as a partridge track. Mom had to see those eagle tracks, and I was proud to show them off. Back up the brook we went.

The trip turned out to be a bummer. Someone had lost a turkey, and it had wandered into my world. We never saw the eagle—or even the turkey.

After a later Libby Brook trip, I told Mom about giant raccoon tracks I had seen—each track as big as both of my two hands. Back up the brook we went. Right then.

Mom's voice and eyes explained what I should know about bears. My "raccoon tracks" were really bear tracks. First, I should never walk toward a bear or get between a mother bear and her cubs. Next, I should always remember that Libby Brook was the bear's home first. I followed Mom's advice and never had bear problems. All the same, wouldn't it be great to have a bear for a pet? It would be fun to scratch those big, black ears.

So you ask, how was the fishing upstream in Libby Brook? It was great. It was a lot easier to fish under Main Street than upstream in the alders, but many days I had Libby Brook upstream all to myself. Mom liked trout.

There's no doubt about this in my mind. My mom saved my life at Libby Brook when I was about twelve years old, and she wasn't even at the event.

Mom loved the outdoors. When her mother's and school teacher's jobs permitted, she walked or snowshoed, depending on the season, sometimes for miles. Sometimes I accompanied her even though my snowshoes were much too small for me. It was fun to discuss the things we saw: trees, wildflowers, birds, animals in summer, and wind-carved snow waves on farm fields and field lines in winter.

One day, perhaps a year before the event, I came home from school and found Mom's snowshoes lying in the yard. Strange. She always kept her cherished webs hanging safely in the shed.

In the kitchen, covered by a blanket, Mom sat shivering at the open door of our wood-fired cook stove. I had never seen fear on Mom's face.

"Mom! What happened?"

"So cold. So cold. So cold," she said. "I fell." She pushed her shaking hands into the warm, open oven. "Bushes along the farm field line held up the snow blanket, but my snowshoes dropped through. They tangled in the bushes and I fell. The snow was so deep and soft that I foundered, and I couldn't get my feet under me to stand up.

"So cold. So cold. It took me a long, long time to unbuckle my snowshoe harnesses so I could stand. It took me a long, long time to refasten my snowshoes to my moccasins again. I just got home a few minutes ago."

Mom slid her chair closer to the stove. She sat staring into the oven. Suddenly she looked at me and said, "Leonard I will go to the hardware store tomorrow and buy snowshoes and harnesses that fit you." Her face lost the fearful look. "You are going to learn to snowshoe safely."

Hey! Mom was back to being Mom again, and I was going to get the snowshoes I'd been bugging her about all winter. I was going to visit the cold, white world with Mom.

I had never had Mom for a teacher. Probably that was arranged. I got along with her because I learned to do sooner what I had to do later anyway. My friends complained (often) that Mom was very impatient. Hey! No sweat. Mom was a piece of cake at home.

However, snowshoes and snowshoeing became a school—and Mom was the teacher. Believe that.

Lesson one: Attach harnesses to the snowshoes SECURELY.

Lesson two: Attach harnesses and snowshoes to my moccasins SECURELY.

Lesson three: Check everything frequently to see that all is SECURE.

Lesson four: While learning, USE ski poles to prevent falls. PERIOD.

Lesson five: Learn to walk with my feet spread apart like I'd wet my pants. (Mom didn't say it quite like that.)

Lesson six: Pay attention to where I'm going and "see" what is under the snow.

Lesson seven: Practice around the house. Around the garden. Around the school yard across the road. AGAIN. MORE.

Much sweat. Hey, my friends are right. Mom is some tough teacher!

When we had time together we snowshoed over farm fields and (carefully) over field lines. I eventually achieved Mom's standard for snowshoe safety, but spring came. We hung our webs in the shed. Not to worry in Aroostook County. Winter returns. Always. The next winter Mom and I enjoyed the white world together, and I often traveled alone.

One day I followed fields and field lines from the end of Brunswick Street (at that time my home in Fort Fairfield) to the gorge through which Libby Brook runs. Wind had blown tons of granular snow from acres of farm fields into a remarkable drift at the top edge of the gorge—perhaps as wide, flat and smooth as a paved, two-lane highway. I followed fox tracks along the smooth edge of the drift. I saw a winter-white rabbit in bushes down along the brook. Wow! I'd have something to tell Mom about.

Today, seventy years more or less later, I vividly remember the next few seconds of that day. A piece of the drift, perhaps thirty feet wide, twenty feet deep, and a hundred feet long dropped under me and started to roll down into the gorge. It sounded like a hushed rumble.

I scurried, ran, scrambled, and clawed up the rolling snow to stay on top. My snowshoes did not fail me. Part way down the gorge the drift fell apart, wedged against bushes, and all was still. I slid off the drift, climbed up the gorge through the gaping hole, and ran onto the flat field. My snowshoes did not fail me.

That afternoon I had more than fox tracks and a winter-white rabbit to tell Mom about. She hugged me. My world became better year after year as I learned more.

However, I had no idea, no idea at all, that Libby Brook, my wonderful world, was due for disaster. After all, what could possibly harm miles and miles of a brook that had developed and lasted for centuries. Nothing. It's just too big to break.

Well, maybe.

World War II was the event that damaged my Libby Brook world. There were no guns or bombs at Libby Brook. There were too many potatoes grown for the war. I heard men talking in my dad's garage about potatoes selling for pennies a barrel. Government money allowed farmers to exist, sort of. It was confusing.

My friends at school told about farmers dumping potatoes—barrels, hundreds of barrels—of potatoes into Libby Brook gorge. We didn't worry. The potatoes didn't roll through bushes and into the brook.

We should have worried. The tons and tons of potatoes froze, thawed, turned into a stinking, gooey, rotten mess and flowed slowly through bushes and into my world, Libby Brook. No kid should have to endure the grief I endured every time I saw and smelled the rotten, stinking potato soup that had become my new world. I didn't visit that world for years.

One day I got my courage up, climbed down Libby Brook gorge and revisited my old world. Wow! The rotten mess was gone—flushed away by years of spring high water—washed clean. I could see trout in the brook. My old world was back. Once in a while I still visit the old place. Libby Brook is a good place.

MEMORIES OF CHILDHOOD
by Norma Ouellette

I was born in Caribou, Maine August 16, 1931. My parents were Tom and Cora Cyr. We lived in a home down a driveway from our grandparents. That, of course, was the Raymond family—my mother's parents and siblings. My great-grandparents had moved into the home also. My great-grandfather Joseph Forgue was born in 1854 and died in 1934. My grandmother Albina Foisy was born in 1857 and died in 1959. In 1949 after being married, when we had our first child, a boy named Steven, we then had a five-generation picture taken. We were all proud of that.

When my great-grandfather became ill, I was about three years old. They took me up to the bedroom where he was lying in bed, ill. He wanted me to kiss him and I wouldn't because he had a big white beard and mustache. That was too bad, now that I think of it. After he died Grandmother Forgue stayed in the Raymond home. Since we were not too far from where they lived, I spent a lot of time with the grandparents, aunts and uncles. There were five boys and eight girls. Some of them had already moved on; I believe there were still five girls and no boys living there at that time.

My memories of my Grandpere Raymond are warm and happy ones. He always seemed to have time for children and he was a great storyteller. Kids would get home from school and say to each other "Hey, Grandpere Raymond is home. Let's go ask for a story." And they would line up on the steps of the front porch and wait for my grandfather. They loved to hear his stories; he just had such a way with finding the interesting stories of life, and taking the time to share them. My memories of him are so wonderful.

Another thing I remember so vividly is that after dinner at the Raymond home, we all had to say the rosary with Grandpere. Sometimes he said it in English sometimes he said it in French, but there was never a time that we did not pray the rosary. *"Au nom du pere et du fils et saint spirit . . ."*

During World War II in Caribou there was an observation tower where volunteers would stand and watch for planes. We never knew if the enemy would make it to our shores, but we knew that if they did, they would likely be heading for the Presque Isle Airbase. My grandmother volunteered as a lookout, even with all the children she had to care for. The steps up to the tower were not regular steps, they were made of metal pipes—more like a ladder, I think. Anyway it wasn't easy to get up to the observation tower and very often my grandmother Raymond would take me with her on her shift. I loved those times. That was when I decided that I wanted to be an airline stewardess. I loved planes. I loved flying. I never got to be a stewardess but I sure traveled a lot.

Now to go on to Grandmother Forgue. She did not speak English. My great-grands were both born in Canada. The Raymond home was an old Victorian with very steep stairs and windows to the floor in some bedrooms. Great-grandmother always took a walk every day around the house. One day I was walking up to see them. Grandma was coming out to walk. She didn't see me, and as she walked around the porch, she put her hand on the railing and jumped over perfectly on the lawn. She did not know that I had seen that. She continued her walk. I believe she was in her 80's then.

Her morning ritual for breakfast was a juice glass with Port wine and a raw egg in it. I did see her break the egg and drop it in the wine.

Of course being very young I didn't know Port wine was a liquor. I don't know how long she did that. Nowadays they say Port wine is good for you. I don't know about the raw egg.

Then one of the family members told me she saw Grandmere sliding down the banister of the very steep stairway. There was only one bathroom and it was at the top of the stairs. I would guess she got tired of walking up and down them. Who knows.

This will be the final tale about Grandmere. One sunny afternoon my mother and grandmother were having their afternoon tea. They were in the dining room that had a big window that looked out to the front lawn. Great-grandmere was upstairs having her afternoon nap. Her window was a tall one and reached the floor. It was open and had a screen. When Grandmere got up she walked through the window to the lawn, which was two stories down. My grandmother saw her sitting on the lawn and said to my mother, "What is Mere doing on the lawn?" When the doctor arrived and checked her out she had no broken bones or bruises. I was told he had to give my grandmother tranquilizers, as she was so upset. No wonder. It was the talk of the town, I believe, and I always felt God must believe in angels.

These are the memories I have of my Great-grandmother. She did live to 102 and we had those pictures of five generations with our first child.

My great-grandmother's maiden name was Foisy. We had a very small family tree with that name. I believe I mentioned she and my great-grandfather came from St. Hilaire, Quebec.

When we moved to New Hampshire I worked for a few years at an antique shop in Milford, NH. This type of shop tends to have customers that come in often, looking to add to their collection. One couple from Massachusetts was in just about every Sunday. They were just friends to each other. I would open cases for him. His collection was old writing pieces like pens, pencils, etc. We never exchanged names. Then one Sunday when they came in I greeted them with *Bon Jour*. The lady turned quickly and said, "You speak French." I answered, "Very little, but I can understand it." She then replied, "I am a French teacher." I asked "What is your name?" She answered, "Claudette Foisy." I quickly explained about my great-grandmother and the small family tree we had. She asked if I would mail her a copy of it. I said of course. She gave me her address and so I mailed it to her. The next week they came in and she said, "Hello Cuz." That was a surprise and quite a nice one.

We kept in touch for a few years. However, the connection stopped and I have no longer heard from her, sorry to say. It is a small world and you never know what you can learn or find. I am sure other people have had the same experience.

Do You Know Ben Davis?
by Rachel Burden

Today you might drive around Aroostook's back roads and spot a few tired sentinels of the past—the apple orchards. Where did they go and why did they leave?

Years ago it was rare not to see a prosperous orchard along with a prosperous farm. My life has now spanned eight decades, so I'm declaring myself an expert on the subject. If you were not lucky enough to live on a farm, you most certainly had an apple tree or two in your backyard.

When you allow yourself to indulge in apple memories of youth, it is amazing how the brain will supply not only the names and locations of your favorite trees, but with the memories come wonderful smells and almost pungent flavors.

We had two orchards on the Ray Higgins farm when I was growing up. The one west of the house had five trees. Favorite of all of us kids in the family was the Sopsy (Winesap) tree. By Ray's firm decree, we were not allowed to climb the tree or shake the tree to get our tasty delights, but we were permitted to have all the windfalls that we could pirate away from the rest of the family. The boys had a distinct advantage early as they slept in a tent all summer not too far from the orchard. We girls probably made the score even, as we could keep an eye on the tree while the boys were in the field. Other trees there included a very big Alexander tree which was perfect for climbing, a small Ben Davis tree with very hard small apples that lasted most of the winter, a Strawberry apple tree, and a Dudley Winters tree. Records show that "Grandfather planted most of the trees that we remember." Ray did buy some Ben Davis trees from a traveling salesman. He advertised them as "the choice luxury apple favored in all fine hotels." Out of twenty purchased, only one survived.

Our larger orchard was between us and the "hired man's house" (Christine McPherson's house now). Close to the field road, there was a row of plum trees. My taste bud memories are teased when I think of the tangy sauce and marmalade my mother used to make. We had Duchess trees, Wealthies, Fameuse, Tetoskies, crab apples (one with large apples, great for crab pickles) and Gideons. Gideons looked like Yellow Transparents from a distance and often people driving by would stop and help themselves. They were all right for cooking, but fearfully sour! The lower fringe of the orchard had a row of small bushes on which you could pick cranberries, currants and chokecherries.

Why would my father destroy such a garden spot? At the time I was sad, sad about seeing the orchard disappear. Coming home from the Old Mill School one day, the funeral pyre greeted my senses. I really did understand the reasons. The trees were older and worms had invaded many varieties. And besides, all that good land could now produce more potatoes. King potato had won out again!

THE OLD ONE REMEMBERS
by Rachel Burden

Some Depression Stories

My sister Mariam reminded me of the time Dad took her to Dr. Lowery, our dentist, for some fillings and took along two dressed chickens to pay the bill.

Apparently 1933 and 1934 were two of the hardest years on the farm. My brother Claude wrote that Dad almost lost the farm and that really shook me up. Being twelve or thirteen then, playing with paper dolls, reading every book in sight, and loving school, I was certainly sheltered from the real world. I do remember hearing Mama and Dad talking in bed one night about the fact that Rachel really needs new shoes and how are we going to manage that? Probably they sacrificed some of their needs and I (Rachel) had new shoes.

The boys had lots of unemployed friends who enjoyed coming to our house. They would gather upstairs in the boys' bedroom to talk and swap! Since few of them had extra nickels in their pockets, one great way to acquire new things was to trade for them. There would be much dickering over tie pins, belts, books, knives, magazines and even some clothing. Sisters were definitely not allowed, but we knew from the laughter that it must be a lot of fun.

Sometimes the sisters were a part of amusements such as mental races. We would take paper and pencil and have races. Who could write all the 48 states and capitals the fastest, or the presidents in order. We had a small jigsaw puzzle made of wood that we assembled over and over. We would time ourselves to see who could finish it the quickest. Sometimes we would take a long word and see who could get the most smaller words out of it in a timed period.

Other Stories from the Old Days

Summer Sundays. Sunday was always a full day. There was no weekend off for Dad or the farm boys, so they attended to the usual chores of milking, cleaning out the stalls, feeding the horses and taking the cows to pasture. But summer Sundays meant that the weekly bath would be in the stream down back. Breakfast was usually milk toast, huge platters of it at both ends of the table. While the boys tended to the separator, Grammy was diligently tending toast, flipping the wire racks filled with the home made bread. Mama made the milk gravy. Each platter had a generous amount of gravy, each slice was dipped in hot water and arranged on the platter. What are the big bowls of red, you ask. Home made cranberry jelly, of course, enough for Irwin to have seconds, thirds and still plenty for all the rest of us. Always there was the cranberry jelly, but we did enjoy strawberries and raspberries in season.

After breakfast we read the Bible. Everyone in the family had a Bible of their own, the daily reading was found and two verses each read until the lesson was finished. Time for prayer was led by Grammy Higgins who pleaded with God for the safety and well being of all the precious ones near and far, mixed generously with thanks and praise to her loving Father. We were all on our knees and prayed the Lord's Prayer together. Visitors to our home were impressed by our morning ritual and in later years spoke of it as a high point in their memory.

Still time before church for Dad to grab the broom and sweep the kitchen floor. Then he was ready for a quick game of hot-jacket. Again it was time to kneel and Dad would be the first IT. Can you guess who swatted your behind? If so you could be the next IT. My mother never played, of course, and she seemed less than enthusiastic about having the girls playing while dressed in Sunday best. "Oh Hazel! It's good for them—will toughen them up."

For the Sunday morning service, we usually tumbled into the Model T, although often Irwin ran just because running was such fun! Since Mama was at the piano, I sat with Dad and Grammy. As I got a little older, I was with Myrtle Dow, Pauline Briggs or Hazel Page. I'm sorry to report that often we were infected with giggles which promised a scowl or a pointed pause from the preacher until we repented.

Sunday dinners were usually Saturday beans warmed up with lots of home made bread and some cookies or cake. The exciting exception was when Dad said he thought we should have a picnic. There would be a fire for boiling coffee and for the steak, maybe fried potatoes or potato salad. Sometimes we just rode around until we found the perfect grassy spot and then later it might be the old mill location near our Chapman farm. On the way back, we certainly would stop at Grammy Fosses for a visit, a walk through her flower garden and treks up and down the path that led to the spring.

Easy Come, Easy Go
by William McConnell

Work was scarce for a teenager in the Depression nineteen-thirties, so when Harry Sutherland offered me a day's work threshing, I was glad to get it. Since it was mid-winter, I put on my heavy sweater, bought that fall from the catalog.

The threshing machine, made of wood and painted red, was set up on the barn floor. Men threw down sheaves from the mow, someone forked them into the front of the thresher, and out the back came the straw, which it was my job to clear away by pushing it out the open doors at the back of the barn. The high-point of the day came when a long-hidden nest of rotten eggs came through the machine; for a few minutes it seemed one could have cut the air with a knife.

At the end of the day, I went home with three dollars; my nearly new sweater so filled with barbed barley spears as to be virtually ruined.

<div align="center">~~~</div>

During the summer of the same year Will Ross had me help Harold Stevens cut some pulpwood trees within easy walking distance of home. The trees were good sized, many heavy-limbed from growing at the edge of an opening. They were sawed down, limbed, topped, and bark peeled off with a tool called a spud.

Anyone who has ever peeled pulp can attest that is a messy, clothes-destroying job. My gloves, pants, shirt and shoes were soon covered with sticky tree sap.

At the end of two weeks I was paid seven dollars, possibly enough to replace my ruined clothes, and a hint that the road to fame and fortune lay elsewhere.

FISHING BASICS
by William McConnell

About the first of April, we began to think about fishing. Out of a thicket of hardwood switches, I'd cut a pole the length of a broomhandle. I might peel the bark off it, perhaps not. I might get impatient with waiting and decide that I should go find a better pole. A trip to the store for a hank of fishline, winding eight or ten feet of it around the tip of the pole, a hook and sinker, a few worms in a can, and the outfit was ready.

Every night after school, as the weather warmed, we would check the lake shore to see if there was enough open water to fish. Starting from where the path from the house hit the lake, we fished the shore along the next quarter-mile. Small trout worked along the shore in high water, looking for food in the grass and leaves, and we caught enough to keep up our interest. A bunch of us wound up at what we called the Bark Wharf, fishing 'til dark. Grandfather set up a competition between my brother Jack and me; the prize, his telescope steel rod, which I won with four or five fish, the largest perhaps a half-pound. The water soon went down and warmed up, ending our fishing for the year.

A memorable trip as we got older was to walk the three miles into Beaver Brook, on an old hauling road behind Fred Stevens' farm. As there were then not that many fishermen, the trip was quite productive. We would have been with an adult who would be packing the necessities for a noon meal—a frypan, some bacon, bread, and a boiling kettle for coffee. A small fire would be built on a sandy spot, the bacon fried, and half-a-dozen small brook trout for each of us fried in the bacon fat. With bread, coffee, and all the fish we could eat—a meal to remember.

POTATOES, YOU SAY?
by Leonard Hutchins

Just about all of us who grew up in Aroostook County have potato stories. Here's one.

After finishing sixth grade in 1942, my mom let me move from town (Fort Fairfield) to a friend's farm to help for the summer. Two of their three sons were away in World War II. (They both survived the war.)

I often worked with my employer and soon to be friend, Mr. Guy Taylor. It was a great summer. Mr. Taylor, then perhaps sixty years old, had a million stories. He often introduced a story with, "You know, Leonard..."

One morning Mr. Taylor and I were walking between rows of potatoes pulling weeds from the crop. "You know Leonard..." he said, and I listened, "about forty years ago right in this field, a friend and I were harvesting the crop. That was before we had mechanical diggers. We used so-called potato hooks."

I have never seen a potato hook, but several people have described them to me as being like a pitchfork with the tines bent to ninety degrees like a garden hoe.

"We hooked potatoes out row beside row down the field. It was hard, boring work. He hooked faster and got ahead. No way would I take that. I hooked harder and got ahead of him. There we went. It's a sport called 'bulling.'"

"Usually we stopped digging when we had picked, I think it was, twenty barrels that wagon held. That wouldn't do. Whoever stopped would soon be out-bulled.

"We worked through dinner and supper time. (In Aroostook, 'dinner' is the noon meal and 'supper' is the evening meal.) The women were, shall we say, 'upset.' There were two overcooked meals on the stove, and a really lot of dirty dishes, some burned on, in the sink.

"When it got dark, the horses knew they were the brightest part of the crew.

"We called a truce, found a pair of kerosene lanterns, and picked the maybe three acres of potatoes. We had to. It was too cold to leave them.

"Well, we got them in about midnight—ahead of the frost, anyway."

PORTAGE BASKETBALL TEAM—1931
by William McConnell

In my sophomore year a basketball team was formed, and we began practice in the Town Hall, a nearly square floor area too small for a regulation court. There were only a few boys to draw on to make up a team and I became center, though I had what was called "lazy eye," poor vision in one eye causing poor depth perception and so poor ability at ball handling. We had uniforms and a schedule of games was arranged with some county schools. Portage had no such thing as a school bus, and as long as the roads were open, various well-wishers with cars carried us to games away. I remember Reggie Bartlett taking some of us to Washburn for what may have been our first game away.

Typically, Washburn court was in the basement of a school building; the ceiling was very low, ruling out any looping long shot. Typically again, familiarity with these individualized courts always favored the home team. At any rate, by allowing the final period to run a little long, the final score was Washburn 100 and Portage 11, possibly the soundest defeat on record. However, using this home court advantage, in just a few years, playing at home Portage produced teams that defeated many of the four year high schools they faced.

Once enough snow had fallen to end auto travel, Crowley, our teacher and coach, having set up a game schedule, hired Victor Jimmo of Ashland to haul the team by snowmobile on a circuit that included Limestone and Fort Fairfield. The machine was completely open; Victor and Crowley sat in front, and probably eight of us sat on two benches lengthwise of the rear, with blankets over our laps. It was usual at the time for the home team to take visitors one by one into private homes for supper, sleep and breakfast. If we were on the road, Crowley would work out an agreement with a restaurant to serve us all the same basic lunch. We all got school letters at the end of the year.

A snowmobile similar to the one used in Portage

A Favorite Christmas Memory
by Rachel Burden

One year at the Haystack Historical Society we were searching for a good Christmas program. Someone suggested that, after our satisfying, wonderful pot luck meal, we all sit around the table and tell our happiest, favorite Christmas memory. For me the suggestion was a joy. I knew immediately what I wanted to share.

The late 20s and early 30s were severe Depression years. My oldest brother was married in 1929. He and his bride were extremely frugal. Christmas for them was a time of home-made gifts—chiefly sewing and carpentry items. The joy of making, decorating, and of baking favorite goodies seemed to satisfy adults, but soon two darling little girls were part of the family circle. Would clothing and rag dolls fill our dreams for the children?

My sister and I were thrilled with the two darling nieces and so when Mama added a workable addition to our Christmas giving we were eager listeners.

"You don't seem to play with your doll carriages much anymore. How would you like to give them to Esther and Phyllis? You know Wallace and Lillian are having a rough time in this Depression. That would give them a great boost."

Wallace painted the carriages and greased the wheels. Lillian made darling quilts, a pillow, sheets and other bedding. Old dolls were rediscovered and dressed delightfully.

Our family gathered at our house on Christmas Eve and the joy of the evening is just impossible to describe. There's a special warm glow that's part of that memory, definitely my *favorite* Christmas memory. The reaction of two little nieces made Christmas a magic holiday that year. Truly it is "better to give than to receive."

CROSSTIES FOR THE RAILROAD
by William McConnell

The winter of 1934-35 my father decided to get a contract to supply crossties to the Bangor and Aroostook Railroad.

Ray Sutherland was a tie-maker, with me as his helper; Dad was the other tie-maker, with brother Jack as his helper. My uncle Ed Randall drove the horse to yard ties out to the landing. In the late fall preparations were made: hay and oats were brought in for the horse, staples for feeding ourselves, saws and axes for making ties, snowshoes for getting around in the snow, a grindstone for sharpening axes, files for sharpening saws. A scoot was built of hardwood to be hitched to the horse to haul ties.

Dad would get up in the dark, build up a fire in the little camp stove, make a pot of rolled oats, mix up a batch of pancakes, and fry them off. We sat down to a breakfast of oatmeal with canned milk split with water, and pancakes with a syrup made of sugar and maple flavoring.

Ed would have been out to the log hovel to feed and water Lady, the mare, her water carried in pails up from the river below.

Dad's pancakes were thin, small enough so eight could fit on his two-cover cast iron griddle. Jack and I each counted on having sixteen of them for breakfast; if, as sometimes happened, we came up short, we could count on being ravenous by ten o'clock.

Baked beans were a staple of the diet: to be sure of a constant supply, I was delegated to go back to camp at lunch-time to build up the fire again to keep the beans cooking. Ed lunched at camp also while the horse ate.

A grub box was stocked each morning to take out to the work site; it held a pail of beans, biscuits, cookies, doughnuts, and molasses gems. At noon a fire would be built up against a big stump, a tea pail hung over the fire to boil, the pail of beans also put on to heat, and the cold biscuits arranged near the fire to warm. Tin plates and cups were filled and the meal eaten quickly before it got cold again in the sub-zero weather. For the same reason there was no lingering after lunch, as the work activity was needed to keep warm. I recall a week or more of thirty-below mornings when, work as fast as I could, I would not be really warm 'til ten.

Each hewer set a goal of twenty-five ties a day. My share of the work with Ray was to take one end of the saw as we cut down a cedar. He then began hewing it into a tie while I sawed the top off a tie already hewed, and carried it out to the road for Ed to load on his scoot for the trip to the landing.

There was a trick to carrying a tie. While on snowshoes, the tie would be stood on the toe of one shoe, big end down. Grasped around the middle, a thrust out with the stomach launched the tie up to balance on one shoulder. Too strenuous a heave meant throwing it on over the shoulder to land buried halfway up its length in the snow behind, too little and it never made it to balance on the shoulder. An icy-butted tie from a three-tie tree took all the moxie that sixteen pancakes provided to get it out to the road. A waist-high fir tree could hold the snowfall on its branches to form a hollow under it. I soon learned not to step too close to a little fir; a slide of the snowshoe down to its base meant a loss of balance and of the tie, and the need to get it up on the shoulder again.

Late in February, it became obvious that we were running out of horse feed, and would have to go to town for more. As luck would have it, we had a two-foot fall of new snow on top of what was there, and a spell of thirty-below nights. The night before we were to leave, Dad snowshoed out a couple of miles toward town, coming back with toes nearly frozen. We started out at daybreak next morning, taking turns snowshoeing ahead to break trail for the horse, up to its belly in the snow, and pulling a light sled. After some five miles we came out into a plowed road and had no more real trouble.

We stopped for a rest and to boil the kettle at ten, lunching again in the middle of the afternoon at Chase Brook, and hitting town at dusk. It seems odd to me now, but I have no recollection of the next two months, especially whether we went back to making ties.

About the time that the ice went out of Portage Lake, a string of boom logs was tied in place at the mouth of the river, and we went up to the landing to start the tie drive. The ties piled on the river bank were tossed into the river, to be carried down to Portage by the current. Two of the youths rode down on individual rafts made by nailing cleats across three or four dry ties. Other than falling off the raft, their only worry was to avoid being swept under a sweeper, a leaning tree jutting out over the water.

I was in the bow of a canoe with Dad; the object was to follow the last of the ties to see that none got hung up in bushes along the bank. I was armed with a pickpole to pull the laggards out into the current again. We got down to the Haysheds, nearly home free, when, in trying to spear a tie, I went overboard into the shallow, ice-cold water, though without serious consequences.

The ties were held in the boom for a few days; finally on a brisk, prevailing breeze the boom was freed, to be carried down the lake by the wind, to the beach at the edge of town. Dad hired several men, the ties were loaded on trucks, hauled to the railroad siding, counted and graded by a buyer for the railroad, and loaded on a railcar.

The whole operation was successful enough so that Dad cut ties again the next winter, with Arthur McCormack in place of Ray Sutherland. The final reckoning on that operation was not as favorable. The railroad was in the habit of letting contracts for more ties than they really needed, as some of the contracts were not filled. The Depression was on, and that year all the contracts were met fully. Faced with a glut of ties, the railroad buyer was very severe in grading. The size and quality of a tie determined the amount paid; down-grading one step resulted in a payment from the railroad that was less than was anticipated.

Without my involvement, these small winter operations continued for several years, one year supplying cedar poles for carrying utility wires.

"I'm Going to Marry Her!"
by Norma Ouellette

I was on my way to the post office in Caribou. I didn't notice the two young men across the way on Sweden Street, but I guess they noticed me. I learned later that these boys were cousins. One turned to the other and declared, "You see that girl over there across the street? Well, I'm going to marry her." I don't know why he said that. We'd never met before. But of course, Roger is the man I *did* marry. It was Roger's cousin who told me that story much later.

Not too long after that, I was with friends rowing on Long Lake near the thoroughfare when we saw a young man standing on the rail of the bridge. It looked like he was going to jump. We all knew the water was too shallow. It wasn't safe. "Don't jump! Don't jump!" we all yelled. But he jumped. He turned his head just as he hit the water and somehow did not break his neck, but scraped from his chin all the way down his belly. He was safe but then needed a lot of attention. My aunt, who was our chaperone, and the rest of us, helped clean him up as best we could. He was a mess! That was Roger.

When Roger and I were married, he was in the National Guard. He was a surveyor and did the surveying for the New York Thruway and the Ohio Turnpike, so we lived for a time in Ohio. Our move from Caribou to Ohio was the first of twenty-five moves during our married life.

Like me, Roger loved flying and he became a fixed-wing pilot and helicopter pilot. He served two tours in Vietnam. Those were difficult years. I don't think any of us believed that we should be in Vietnam. But when you get orders to do something, and you're in the military, you do it. We lived in Hawaii where I learned to do the Hula. The native-Hawaiians said that I was the best "Haole Hula dancer!" (Which is their word for non-native. It is not a derogatory term.)

We lived in South Carolina for a while where I developed my southern drawl and I can still converse with southern people on the telephone. One lady from Comcast called me to help straighten out a billing error and she said "Mz Naama . . . may I call you Mz Naama?" I don't know how she knew I was a Southerner. That was when I was living in Maine. Maybe I had a knack for languages, because I picked up accents quite easily wherever I lived.

We settled in New Hampshire, because that was where my husband was last stationed when he retired. We had a lot of friends in New Hampshire. Vietnam never left Roger, though. He died from the effects of Agent Orange in a VA hospital in 2007 at the age of 78.

When my house burned in September 2015, I looked for a retirement home and decided to move back to the Caribou area where my brother and sister-in-law and family live. I haven't regretted it.

One thing I do regret is that in the fire, we lost all my husband's research and his writings on Acadian history. He had spent years on it, and now it's all gone. When I add his name to the dedication of this book, it will be in memory of the writing that he did so many years ago.

Learning about Hard Work
from Zelma Naomi Smith Lovely
(1882-1943)
by Maxine Lovely Smith

My mother's advice to my sister and to me when we were approaching the age of marrying was "Never, never get married and moved in with your mother-in-law. No house is big enough for two women."

She told us about a time when, as newlyweds, she and dad lived with his parents on their farm in Mapleton. An arrangement was made for him to work in the woods with his father for wages, while she would do housework for his mother to earn board and room for the two of them. Mom had probably not worked terribly hard at home, as she had two older sisters. However, she had "worked out" for other families in her neighborhood when she was younger, and did know that one must work hard to earn even the meager wages paid for household help in those years.

The work that this new bride had married into was not what she had expected. Her mother-in-law would call her as early as 3:30 on Monday mornings, saying, "Velma, you have overslept." This early hour was to get a head start on her neighbors so Grammie would have her wash on the line before they had hung theirs. A huge boiler of water would be heated all night on the wood fire, and in the morning, the white clothes were put in to boil awhile, which would make them whiter. Then they must be forked out into cold rinse water, wrung dry, and hung outside—all before most of the other family members were out of bed. Tuesdays meant ironing all day using irons heated on the wood stove. Everything had to be ironed! Dad was the eldest in the family of eight children, and all their clothes were starched and ironed: blouses (called shirtwaists), dresses, shirts, pants, aprons, even underwear, pillowcases, sheets, and yes, dishwipers, had to be ironed and neatly stacked in drawers. Every day of the week had its special work to be accomplished. The "hired girl" was expected to do all this, as well as cook, get hearty meals, clean, make beds, wash dishes, and do any other chores that needed to be done. Mom found herself in that impossible position, and she resented it. Luckily, her hated job ended about six months later when she and Dad moved into a house on a farm of their own.

My Grandmother Zelma Lovely was a hard taskmaster. I'm sure she had worked hard too, as a young woman; but as I remember her, she usually was sitting in her big Boston Rocker in the kitchen overseeing all that went on. Her thin wispy hair was white and straight, and thick glasses made her dark brown eyes appear huge. She was short, stout, proud, haughty, a bit vain, impressed by wealth and affluence, and lacking in her concern for the less fortunate. Her own younger children were spoiled and not ambitious. Even when they had grown older and should have had summer work, they spent the time at home, living as guests. I think perhaps Gram felt that work was demeaning, and that her own children were too good for that.

One day she said to me, "You may think that I am lazy, but I worked hard when I was young, probably too hard. Your grandfather retired when he wasn't yet sixty, and I decided if he wasn't going to work, neither would I! So now I hire a girl to do the heavy work that I no longer can do."

She was usually looking for hired help, and when I became old enough, she would hire me whenever I had a day off from school. Money was so scarce that I would go, even when I knew the unreasonable amount of work to be done. Wages were generous, at one dollar a day, but I was expected to stay overnight in order to be there early enough to get started before daylight.

Gram was not harsh or cruel to me. In fact, I often thought that I was her favorite granddaughter. She told me once that I looked a lot as she did when she was young. Her obsession was to have more accomplished than was humanly possible, and often I would leave at the end of the day before all the work she had planned was finished. This did not upset her. She would say, "Well, we know where we will start next week, don't we?" I was often very tired at day's end, and her remark might be, "Well dear, you will sleep good tonight. A good day's work is good for you."

Looking back, I suspect that she felt benevolent in allowing me to earn the needed money. I was grateful, even for such a hard job, as I could not have gone beyond high school unless I had earned money for clothes. Perhaps she was right about hard work being good for me, and my present good health may be partly a result of such effort in my youth.

Gram had a severe stroke in her late fifties, when I was a senior in Normal School. She was an invalid for many months. I recall visiting her when she was shut in, and she seemed pleased. She said, "We had some good times when you worked for me, didn't we?"

I had to admit the memories were good. I had learned a lot from her. I learned to be kind and more considerate of any help that I employed later in my own household. I also know that we can put off until tomorrow what does not get done today. Grammie Zelma is one grandparent that I remember with mixed emotions.

Toboggan on a Ski Jump
by Norma Ouellette

I was about sixteen years old when a friend said, "Let's go over to Presque Isle to Quoggy Joe to use the toboggan slide." So a group of us went over and I planned on going down the slide with three other girls. I would ride in back. But a man said, Norma, you're too small to go down like that. "You'll fall off and really get hurt. I'll ride on the back to give you some stability.

We started down that toboggan slide. It was a cold day and the snow had been well packed so it was very slippery and in no time we were going so fast it felt like we were flying. What we didn't know was that at the end of the slide someone had built a ski jump. When we hit that our toboggan was actually airborne! It seemed like a very long time before we touched down—hard—on that pond! And of course we continued to fly, but then on ice, for quite a stretch. We tumbled every which way, but if that man had not been on the back I truly would have been hurt seriously. I only weighed about ninety pounds at the time.

OUR 1 MILE WIDE, 6 MILE LONG SKATING RINK
by William McConnell

For an all too brief period in late fall, early winter, we had skating. The quality and duration varied from year to year. Usually there would be a snowstorm just at the time of freeze-up; the wet snow floating in the water formed an off-white, rough ice. By the time the ice was 2 inches thick, we were all over the lake. I even skated one late afternoon up the river to the Haysheds and back, where Eddie Strong and his wife were living in a log cabin, a distance of sixteen miles. I can remember only one year when the ice froze without any snow in it. Taking on the color of the water beneath, the ice was so black that there was the illusion of standing on the surface of the water. This black ice was so hard that my dull skates could hardly get a grip, tending to slide out from under me.

With no money for an item used for so short a season, skates were hard to come by. The first skates at hand were a pair of my father's that had a wooden body and steel runners. Designed to be used on leathersoled boots, they had an upright screw to be turned up into the heel leather, and straps for the toe. With no proper boots, these skates saw little usage. Next were skates modeled after roller-skates, to be clamped to the shoe-sole. We seldom had that kind of shoe. The most successful outfit was made up of a pair of hand-me-down log driving boots of my father's that had leather soles, to which skates were attached with a number of screws to hold them firmly in place.

A bonfire was an essential part of the skating experience, especially at night. There was something magical about leaving the light of the fire to skate out into the darkness for a while before returning to the sociability around the fire.

But a fire could have its problems; on one occasion a container of used motor-oil, put on the fire, exploded, spraying burning oil. Fortunately no one was hurt, but footwear taken off to put on skates was damaged by hot oil spray.

After hours spent on the ice, changing back into frozen boots could present a problem. Already chilled through, hands bared to remove skates and attempt to don boots quickly became clumsy. I can recall a couple of times when I had to make my way home still wearing skates, and remember the pain as my hands warmed again.

Skating everywhere on the lake was too good to last, and soon the ice would be covered by snow. Then we all set-to and cleared a rink, a circle as big as our ambition and the snowfall allowed. Skating in a circle was still fun, and on a bright, sunny weekend we might be joined by some of the grown-ups. Another fall of snow put an end to skating for the year.

Old-Time Potato Picking
by William McConnell

One fall, Dad, Jack, and I picked potatoes for Will Ross. The fields were in Buffalo. Sometimes we rode to work with Will in his Essex; when the fields were below the road and nearer the railroad we walked up the tracks to the fields. We got up in the dark, Dad would fix us some hashed potatoes, put up a lunch, and we would walk up tracks to be at the field at full daylight. We were paid six cents a barrel; yield was lower than became typical in later years as more fertilizer came to be used; the soil was poor and soon ceased to be farmed at all.

All my picking was behind a horse-drawn engine digger; at first the full barrels were loaded on a wagon, not too difficult as the bed of the wagon was low. In later years, trucks came into use, from the 1930 Chevrolet, holding twenty barrels, that Abel Cormier drove, to trucks of gradually increasing capacity. A loader walked along with the truck, and all the men pickers were expected to take one side of the full barrels and help load—not so easy now as the truck bed was higher off the ground.

I picked one fall for my Uncle Mark, boarding with the family and earning forty dollars. My Aunt Sadie went to J.C. Penney and bought a suit, a rather fuzzy blue material, and yellow shoes, and brought them along when they brought me home, to find that Mother had bought a suit from the catalog, a nice looking hard-finished oxford serge, and black shoes, saving me from dressing like a mid-western hick, but putting Sadie to the trouble of returning her purchases.

PRE-DEPRESSION DANCING
by William McConnell

This was the hey-day of the dance pavilion; The Silver Slipper, Two Ginn's Pavilions, Paul's Arena, all scattered along near the Canadian Border south of Fort Fairfield. Lou Michaud formed an orchestra called 'Louie Boy and His Vagabonds', with Lou on violin, his brother Leon on piano, Doug Grant on trombone, and others that played in these dance halls.

In the late twenties, a unit of the Grange was formed in Portage. They built a hall for meetings; there was a kitchen in the basement, with tables for holding pot-luck suppers, and upstairs, a large open area with a hardwood floor for dancing.

As seems to happen with such groups, there was a constant effort to pay on the building loan. Besides suppers, dances were held quite often, the music supplied by Johnny McGowan on drums, and Mildred Dunn playing piano. They would come in from Ashland, play all evening, be faced with the ten mile ride home, all for perhaps a total of ten dollars, though that may have represented most of the ticket sales.

I used to go to the Grange Hall dances, but had no one to teach me the dance steps, and most of my attempts to get a partner were turned down, as I suppose it was obvious that I didn't really know how to dance. My grandfather would put on his suit, buy a pack of inexpensive cigars, and circulate, enjoying the break from his work routine.

High Landing Idyll
by William McConnell

The falls of '33 and '34 I spent at High Landing camp, hunting with Dad and his sports from Lynch's. Commander Holmes was there, Bill Shillings, a conductor for the Pennsylvania Railroad, Joe Shilosky, an engineer for the railroad, Gardiner, Jim and Kenny.

They would arrive on the train. Dad would meet them and bring them up the river to camp. If the water was low, he would put the men out at the Haysheds, to walk the tote-road to camp, while he poled his canoe up the river with their luggage. Larry Robinson and I were already there.

We all hunted from spotted trails that fanned out from camp, leading up into the surrounding ridges. Bird season started on October 1st. For a couple of weeks we walked the tote-road early frosty mornings, hunting partridge. We made trails, got in wood, and got things ready for the deer hunters. Deer season started October 15th, and we could count on some fine fall weather before snow came to stay, a signal for the Ohio party to leave.

I tend to romanticize the time spent at camp. As the hunters left in the early morning, still on the table were the breakfast dishes for ten to twelve men to be washed. On baked bean night I would have to stay in camp all day to keep a fire and tend the bean pot. Memory of such chores quickly faded, while the enjoyment of the hunting experience endured.

Curtiss-Wright Flying Boat
by William McConnell

In the mid-1930s my summer friend Bud and I took a rowboat off the beach without asking. Each taking an oar, we cruised up and down the lake shore. That summer there arrived on the lake a Curtiss-Wright Flying Boat aircraft. Apparently the two pilots were trying to demonstrate to the Maine Fire Department that a plane would be useful in spotting and fighting forest fires. They took my father up for a flight over his district, and moored in a sheltered cove of the lake for several days, where Bud and I examined it from our rowboat.

Later that summer, they wrecked the plane on a submerged reef in a lake down-state, and both pilots drowned. Planes are routinely used today to look for fires; these men were before their time.

A year or two later, a flying boat out of Rockland landed in the lake with engine trouble. Another identical plane flew repair parts and a mechanic up from Rockland, and while repairs were being made, offered rides. For five dollars each, my father and I were taken for a short hop up over the upper end of the lake—my first plane ride.

As We Became *Adults*

THE HOPECHEST
by Maxine Smith

Most girls in the days of my growing up spent a lot of time thinking about whom they should marry. My parents, somewhat modern for their generation, expected us all, including the girls in the family, to go on after high school for more education. My mom would often tell my sister and me how important it was for us to be trained, in case we ever had to earn our own living. However, that plan for career did not cancel out the fact that we also would eventually be getting married and having our own family.

I soon learned that nice girls should *never* be in obvious pursuit of a man; yet we were definitely expected to be in silent lookout for a suitable husband. Those girls who didn't choose to marry were never given credit for wanting to make a go of life on their own, but were quite stigmatized with the common conclusion that no man had ever asked her to be his wife. Thus came the term, "Old Maid," to describe any and all single women of marriageable age in the village.

Because we as young girls were expected, and looked forward, to be married someday, there was passed along the custom, or the accepted practice, of each daughter starting a "hopechest." This might be a trunk, a wooden box, or even a large cardboard box where precious things could be safely stored. High school girl graduates were commonly given beautiful cedar chests for graduation gifts to be used for such storage and also as a piece of furniture in a new home. This chest would hold items prepared by our own busy hands, or purchased with our own scarce funds; items to be used in our new home to be established with that very special young man who would mysteriously appear on his white horse and sweep us off our feet. Mothers taught their daughters to create uniquely decorated towels, embroidered pillowcases, sheets, table cloths, fancy doilies, and later, when working for a wage, to collect small kitchen tools to add to this stash.

As a small girl, I learned to embroider and was given a set of seven linen dish wipers, with a stamped design on each one showing the days of the week. I learned to make small, even stitches, outlining scenes of activities for each day; washday on Monday, ironing on Tuesday, and so on. It was a common form of crafting then, and we were encouraged to do our very best work on each one. My memory is of the number of times my mother urged me to get the towels and other crafted items out of my box and show them to grammies, aunts, or friends who were always generous with their praise. I also recall using those fancy dish towels and embroidered pillow cases when, after my knight on his white horse arrived and rescued me from my spinsterhood, I started "keeping house."

Many skills were learned and precious dreams created in the plans made while we girls were filling our hopechests. Perhaps the planning ahead for so long and so seriously for future life with our loved one did help to make the marriages of that day more solid and lasting.

Making Maple Syrup
by William McConnell

One spring my mother and I made maple syrup. Some work had been done the fall before; a big boiling pot had been made of the bottom half of a steel drum, its hanging bail made of strands of telephone wire, the woods version of the farmer's haywire. A supply of dry wood was ready, a dozen gallon tin cans had been given bails ready to hang on whittled out wooden spiles. It remained to bore ¾ inch holes in ten or a dozen sugar maples, drive in the spiles, and hang the pails. An arrangement of three chest-high upright posts and a horizontal pole passed through the bail of the boiling pot allowed it to be moved on and off the fire. We had a 20 gallon garbage can for sap storage and were soon in business. The fire was located in front of an Adirondack

Shelter built years before, a comfortable place to sit and some shelter from the weather. A fresh fire and boiling was started each morning, with more sap added from time to time until mid-afternoon. The next two hours reduced the boil to half a water pail, carried back to camp to be boiled on the kitchen stove to syrup stage as judged by Mother. Too thin and it wouldn't keep, too thick and it would start to turn to sugar.

It would soon be time to expect fishermen as guests at ice-out. We had made enough syrup for our own use, so ended the boiling, dumping the full garbage can of sap, as we were collecting it faster than we could boil it down. Mother later traded a gallon of syrup with a woman for a gallon of strained honey.

FEEDING THE MEN
by Phyllis Hutchins

I remember that our table was very often very busy. During the Depression years, hobos (not tramps) walked the Canadian Pacific Railroad tracks which were between our farm and the Aroostook River. They were gentlemen—jobless only because of the times—and they would do whatever needed to be done for a meal. Whether we needed work or not, mother fed them. Also there were crews of neighbors who came to help cut ice, cut wood and harvest crops. Neighbor women came to help mother cook, and she in turn went to help them when it was their turn.

My turn to feed a crew came in the 1960s. We had just moved to out-of-the-way Oxbow, Maine. A logging boss, Ronald Fournier, asked if I would feed his truck drivers because a diner was so far away. Since I was not a professional, I hesitated. "Hey, look Phyllis," the good-natured fellow coaxed, "Leonard and your kids look pretty well fed." I finally accepted a very satisfying job. Those boys always grinned and wiped their feet when they came in, ate everything in sight, and never failed to thank me when they left. Sometimes they brought their friends.

A Drink of Gin
by William McConnell

My father had, for a number of years, guided deer hunters for V. E. Lynch, at the forks of the Machias River. Early in the thirties, Lynch retired and closed the camp, perhaps as a result of the Depression. The hunters that Dad had been guiding were left without a place to hunt, and Dad came up with the idea of building a camp at High Landing on Fish River, an area familiar from his earlier logging days. This had two double bunks that could sleep eight men, but after a year, Dad decided to build another sleeping camp.

Sometime in March, a bunch of us left Portage on foot to go to High Landing to build this cabin. We had two sleds, shod with four inch wide runners, with fills to pull and steer in front, and a push-pole in back. On the sleds were our personal gear, food for our stay, and what building supplies were needed. We had about a fifteen mile trip ahead, and made good time, as there was a good crust on the snow. Besides Dad and me, Zeph and Ernest Prosser were along.

At the camp site, fir trees were cut down nearby, logs skidded to the work area, peeled with a drawshave, and the walls logged up. The roof was covered with cedar splits, made on the spot. Openings were cut out for windows and a door, and the floor boarded in.

Toward the end of our stay, on a Sunday, the men decided to go into Ferguson Pond to ice-fish. Zeph struck off through the woods. We were on snowshoes, and after a couple of miles we hit the pond. Someone made a hole or two for fishing, and a place was cleared down to the ground to build a lunch fire. By then a light rain was falling, and soon after lunch, fishless, we snowshoed back to camp. I came down with a cold, and fainted when I got out of bed and stood up. Dad's concern prompted him to concoct for me a mug of his cure-all—a hot, sweet drink, laced with gin.

Teaching John
by Leonard Hutchins

John isn't his real name, but he was a real kid. He lived near a lot of woods. Not acres. Square miles of woods.

He was a shy boy. He talked to his classmates only when necessary. Teachers? Just about never if he had his way. I was a teacher at Ashland Community High School, so John's shy personality was my problem. I thought students should feel free to talk with teachers. My, "Good morning, John," earned me only a quick nod and nervous sideways glance as he scooted down the hall. Other teachers had no better luck with John.

However, one morning before classes I heard one student say to another, "Hey, John caught another marten."

Wow! Why didn't I think of that? I did a little marten trapping, so John and I had something in common. Incidentally, marten pelts sold for about $20 at that time. John might have been the wealthiest kid in school.

Next morning I found John sitting alone in the cafeteria waiting for the first bell to ring. "John," I said. His eyes bugged out. He was cornered—by a teacher. "I use #110 Conibears. Would you tell me what kind of trap you use for marten?"

His mouth dropped open a little, and he cocked his head to one side. Perhaps a full minute later he said, "You trap marten?" It took him another minute or so to realize he hadn't answered my question. "Oh. Yeah. I use #110 Conibears too. Hey, what do you use for . . ." some time later the bell cut our conversation short.

"Hey, Mr. Hutchins," John said the next morning when I found him waiting for me in the cafeteria. "You know it's good to have my father tell me I'm smart and he's proud of me, but . . ."

As a teacher I was proud of myself. John had started a conversation—and with a teacher no less.

"One day last year," John continued, "I was walking my trap line maybe three miles from home when I met up with a set of tracks that didn't belong there. Strange. I knew I was the only one trapping in that swamp. Out of curiosity I followed those tracks. In another mile or so I met up with two sets of tracks together.

"Whoa! This can't be, I thought. I followed the two sets of tracks far enough to know they were my tracks—I was going in a circle. This can't be. I was lost—right in my own backyard. I didn't carry a compass. Why did I need a compass in my own backyard? It was a cloudy day, so I didn't have the sun for direction. How stupid can I be? Stupid enough to get lost without a compass. And I didn't have any lunch either.

"I built a fire and waited for Dad. I knew he'd come and bail me out; and I expected him to give me grief for being so stupid."

"John," Dad said when he found me about suppertime. "I'm proud of you. You did exactly right. You stopped when you realized you were lost. John, you are a smart boy."

"You know what? I think I was pretty stupid to get lost right in my own backyard."

It has been maybe 50 years since John told me about that event. How could I forget?

Lost Hunter and a Lesson
by Leonard Hutchins

Poor guy. He knew how to hunt in the woods. He did everything right, but he still got lost. He was embarrassed.

I didn't know this fellow from Caribou, but that didn't matter. People who live and work in the woods, even part-time, take time to find someone who doesn't show up as planned.

My connection to the woods was that my wife, Phyllis, and I had recently acquired Oxbow Hunting Lodge and Dining Room. When our game warden, Maurice Gordon, knocked on the kitchen door one dark night looking for help and a loud rifle, I joined him.

The lost hunter's partners were waiting in their car parked by Houlton Brook on the Oxbow Road. They had not heard a single shot from their lost friend.

"Stand still, listen, and try to determine the direction if he answers our shot," Maurice told the hunters. "Point in that direction."

"Go up the road fifty yards or so and shoot once," Maurice instructed me.

I loaded my .30-06 rifle and walked up the road, pointed the rifle straight up, held the butt firmly against my shoulder, and pulled the trigger. A basketball-sized ball of orange flame exploded from my rifle barrel, and the butt slammed down against my shoulder.

We stood still in the dark. Waited. Listened. "Come on," I thought.

Whump. That's him. I thought the sound came from a long ways up Houlton Brook. The others agreed.

"You fellows stay here with the car in case he walks out," Maurice instructed the hunting partners.

"We'll go in and pick him up if he stays put," he said to me. "And please don't fire signal shots that will confuse me," he added to the hunters.

This event happened, I think, forty-odd years ago. Why I remember that I thought Maurice was optimistic for our chances for a quick success, I don't know. At least I had the sense enough to keep my mouth shut.

We floundered in the dark what seemed like miles up Houlton Brook when Maurice said, "There is a beaver dam just up here we can cross. I don't want to wade the brook."

"Wow," I thought, "if there really is a beaver dam up here, this guy really knows this country—night or day." There really was a beaver dam, and we crossed the brook dry.

"Leonard," Maurice said, "fire a signal shot so we can get a better line on him."

I shot again and he returned an immediate answering shot.

We floundered a few hundred more yards, and there through the thick trees I saw a fire glow. I jogged a few steps toward the hunter— lost no more.

"Leonard, wait." Maurice said. He caught up to me. "If our man is a nervous guy and we run at him at night, he might think we are bears. And he's got a gun."

It occurred to me that I'd have somewhat to learn if I were to be a game warden.

Our man wasn't nervous. He thanked us for coming and said his compass seemed just plain wrong. He believed it anyway and got lost.

Upon checking his compass with Maurice's, our hunter found his compass was 180 degrees off. The polarity was reversed. He had been welding and guessed that strong magnetic fields had done the bad deed.

"Well," Maurice said, "there is a woods road a couple hundred yards south of us. A half-mile east on that will take us to Route 11. About a mile north of that will take us back to the Oxbow Road, and a half-mile east will get us to Houlton Brook. If there are no more lost hunters we might get some sleep tonight." He chuckled. I wondered if all game wardens had a strange sense of humor.

I also wondered if Maurice really knew all of the directions and distances he described.

A couple hundred yards down south of us there was, indeed a woods road. A half-mile east took us to Route 11. He really did know his way around the woods—day or night.

"Wow!" Maurice said when he reached Route 11 and looked south. "We're in luck. There is a vehicle coming. We'll get a message back to Houlton Brook, and they will come after us. We don't really need that walk."

We all saw the glow over a hill south of us. We waited. Two minutes. Five minutes. No vehicle. "Come on," I coaxed our "ride."

"Oh no!" Maurice said when a fact dawned on him. "That's not a vehicle. That's lights on a way station for either the electric company or the telephone system."

Tired as we were, we walked. North back to the Oxbow Road. West back to Houlton Brook. The Caribou hunting party, thankful to be reunited, left for home. Maurice drove me back to Oxbow Lodge and left—for who knows where.

Maybe he had another hunter to find. He could do it.

Since that time, every time I travel that area, I remember the night Maurice taught me a lesson about the Maine Woods.

REUBEN, REUBEN, I'VE BEEN THINKING
by William McConnell

How do you feel about feeding the birds? A pleasant recreation for many; the only warning commonly heard is not to start feeding in the fall unless you are prepared to continue all winter, as the birds could starve if feeding stops.

In three summers, Sis has named Reuben and Rachel and tamed the loon pair residents of "our" pond. Running the outboard from the wharf to her favorite fishing spot, she'd sit by the hour, fishing with some worms for trout. A by-product was a limitless supply of chub, killed and thrown out for the loons, who would come from anywhere in the pond at the sound of the outboard starting, to park twenty feet from the boat and wait for a hand-out. Or rather the more daring Reuben would; Rachel was more timid, staying farther away. Coming from someone who can't tell one from another, this sounds chauvinistic. Let's just say that the more aggressive of the two was given the name of Reuben. Sis claims that she got Reuben to take a fish from her fingers by holding it under water. It was a new experience for the rest of us to watch Reuben swim by and under the boat about a foot under water and clearly visible.

The last time I tried fishing with live minnow as bait, I had to splash water at Reuben with the paddle to make him keep his distance. There was a chance he would take a fish while it was still on the hook. (Have you heard stories of this happening? Dave says he caught a "short" trout on worms on his lake. He cut the line and it was swallowed by nearby loon, embedded hook and all.)

Sis would have a few chub to bring back to the wharf. Calling him by name, she would entice Reuben near, tossing the fish to demonstrate his tameness. Shortly, anytime there were people on the wharf for whatever reason, he would come sailing up, looking for action.

The next step was to keep the minnow trap set so that a chub supply would be available to show visitors and guests, camcorder at the ready, Reuben's antics. He'd be out thirty feet watching. Seeing a fish tossed six feet from the wharf, he would dive and take it under the water, a big swirl marking the spot, apparently swallowing the fish while still underwater, as the bigger the fish the longer he'd be down.

We *do* see other boats on the pond occasionally; what are they to make of loons that come up near their boat and hang around? One cannot always see the end result of following the impulse to get more involved with wild creatures. It might be best to let them fend for themselves.

A Winter at Tracks' End
by William McConnell

In January and February of 1943, my father and I worked as pulpwood scalers for the Great Northern Paper Company (GNPCO) at St. Francis, Maine. The buildings of the town are rather scattered out, on a road that runs along the St. John River, with a pocket of activity at the railroad station; and further along, a general store, movie theater, and church provide the nucleus for another grouping. We had a bedroom in a private home a half-mile or more from work, and ate in a cookroom set up by GNPCO in an empty house nearer the station.

We were doing a hauling scale on eight or ten trucks that were bringing in loads from the previous summer's cutting operation about thirty miles upriver from town, over a winter road that ran mostly in the river bed. GNPCO had in use two tandem-wheeled trucks holding about five cords; these were in use around the clock, with different drivers. The rest of the fleet was made up of converted farm trucks, with taller stakes and sideboards instead of the usual rig for hauling potato barrels. These trucks varied in capacity from three to four cords, and made two trips a day. They drove empty the thirty miles to the yards, hand-loaded a series of piles across the truck width, and on their return, backed up to the side of a freight car and off-loaded the wood. Our scale was used to pay the truckers.

There was a small scaler's shack at the siding where we took turns sleeping at night, to be aroused periodically to scale the two GNPCO trucks working through the night and to fire up the stove with peeled, dry, pulpwood we had sawed in two with a bucksaw. We had the further duty of checking that full freight cars were leveled off on top, that no ends stuck out needing to be sawed off, and that bills of lading were filled out for shipment to Millinocket.

Everything went smoothly for a couple of weeks. Then, Don Swan, in charge of the whole operation, told us that the mill scaler had reported that our scale was running 2% greater than his, with the inference that we should adjust our scale down to compensate. A farm truck typically held four piles, the highest next to the cab and graduating downward toward the rear. The piles were somewhat rounded, end to end, and the slack in the stakes allowed the piles to be longer at the top than at the bed of the truck. Allowance had to be made for the boxes over the rear wheels. Altogether, scaling such a load becomes a rather subjective task, with no two scalers necessarily coming up with the same precise amount.

On my first attempt to revise my scale down a little, I struck a snag. The truck owner, having hauled for days, was well aware of what his scale should be, based on what he had been getting every trip, and protested my scale, even getting Swan to scale the load. I had the very uncomfortable feeling of being caught in the middle, unable to satisfy either GNPCO or the truckers, and felt like quitting. My father took Swan aside, reminded him that his first priority was to get the pulpwood out to the railhead in the two months that the winter road would be stable; that to antagonize the truckers enough that they quit hauling would be far more serious than the little matter of a 2% difference in scale.

We all went back to business as usual, and had no more trouble. But the episode illustrates what I have come to accept as a character defect, in that I am thin-skinned, and would rather take flight than fight.

TREADING THE BOARDS
by William McConnell

After my high school graduation I was at home for the winter. As a means of raising money to support the church, the Ladies Aid each month put on some sort of public affair; often a church supper, but that winter it was popular to put on a play. Pastor Swank was behind a play in which I played the part of a French detective. In another play I was the husband of Roseanne Frazier; this was a play that a church-going audience would not find objectionable, and we were asked by the Men's Club at Ashland to put it on there. Then came the call to go to Masardis for another showing.

The next play was built around a traveling circus, with a raid on the girlie show by the local sheriff—an audience pleaser but a radical change from what we had been presenting, and when the Ashland group asked for a return engagement, they didn't know what they were getting into. At the Portage showing, Ray Sutherland and others helped things along by getting a drink into Cecil Brown, who played the sheriff so broadly that things almost got out of hand.

The season wound up with a play sponsored by the Catholic Church; I was in it but further details escape me beyond the hug to quiet her nerves that Silvia Tanguay gave me just before the curtain went up.

How Dry I Am
by Rachel Burden

How Dry I Am, How Dry I Am, Nobody Knows, How Dry I am. From birth (almost) I have known that alcohol is a vicious enemy. I think people looked at the new infant and declared excitedly, "She would make a good "Carrie Nation!" And so the training began!

All of my female relatives on the Foss side were members of the WCTU (Women's Christian Temperance Union). The most ardent, strongest, vocal and evangelistic was my Great-Grammy Mac (Mariam McGlauflin). In the book I wrote about her, I included several of her great poems where she put Demon Rum in a corner and shook her finger at him.

The WCTU had an organization for children called the LTL (Loyal Temperance Legion). My sister Mariam and I joined after learning a stern "never, never" pledge. Our leader was Mrs. B., a lady who had an alcoholic husband. (I never knew that until years later). Mrs. B. was my Sunday School teacher.

When I was in seventh grade, I entered an essay contest; topic was "Why Rule G is Necessary." It had to do with the need for abstinence for railroad engineers. I won the dollar and used it to buy my first *personal* Bible. The contest was WCTU sponsored.

I faithfully obeyed my Never, Never pledge, all through high school and college. About age twelve, I began to attend Baptist School of Christian Training for two weeks each summer. There was always a wonderful choice of courses, but my favorite was the alcohol education one, taught by Frederick W. Smith, head of the Maine Civic League. He was Welsh, with an inspiring fervor for the Lord and for teaching us about alcohol and the problems it causes. After three summers, I graduated, took three years post-grad., came back as story-teller teacher (one course), as tent mother at meetings. Later for two summers I taught the alcohol course.

After one year of teaching school, The Civic League called me, asking me if I'd be interested in attending a summer school at Yale on alcohol education and they would pay all the bills. *Terrific Shock! Why me?* But my "Yes" was fast coming. (It was either 4 or 6 weeks. I can't remember.)

The education from people I mingled with was really earth-shaking for this naive farm girl from Aroostook County who didn't know beans about the real world. I was constantly amazed, shocked, horrified, unbelieving and a little scared. My room-mate was Alma Field who worked for Calvert Distilleries in Kentucky. In our group, there were social workers, pastors, priests, AA members, doctors, nurses, police, etc.

Coming back from Yale, The Civic League asked me to speak at some local churches. One of the things I remembered telling folks, was about attending an AA meeting where most everyone was smoking, but eager to give a testimony about God's goodness!

Fred and I were married June 14, 1948. We had been home from our honeymoon only a few days when we had a call from the Civic League asking us to be delegates to an important gathering in Indiana. They would pay for everything and asked us to pick up a young trainee in Portland and take him with us. Fred had not yet settled on a job. A second honeymoon—why not? Fred was an important lay-reader in the Episcopal Church and I had background in alcohol education. We made no promises, but accepted their offer. Out to "Beautiful Lake Winona" with our young passenger was fun. Bruno Caliandro and Fred were a comedy team and laughter was our music all the way.

Homer Rhodeheaver, a famous hymn writer, was our host and he and his sister gave us a tour of their very lavish house, (sunken black bathtub and all)! The opulence and the messages we heard, sometimes seemed at odds.

Fred and I did several church services in the County after coming home, then despite the Civic League job offer, he chose teaching.

Happy Ending!

How dry I am!

Loyal Temperance Union Pledge
Maple Grove Grammar School (1940-1944)

I promise, God helping me,
Not to buy, drink, sell, or give
Alcohol Liquors
While I Live.

From all tobacco
I'll abstain and never
Take God's name in vain.

Shared by Donna Pelletier and Marilyn Chase in memory of their favorite teacher, Mr. Abernathy, a wonderful educator, talented musician, gracious guide through LTL learning of Roberts Rules of Order and himself a doomed alcoholic.

Wedding day, Joyce and Arnie Davis

Our Wedding Day
by Maxine Lovely Smith

Vaughn and I were married just seventy-three years ago, when weddings were more sedate and not much like the glamorous, sometimes showy events we attend today. Here in Aroostook County, where money has never been plentiful, couples were often married very quietly, even in another town. The bride's parents would frequently hold a reception for the newlyweds later in their home.

People were seriously concerned with the war effort in 1943. Gasoline was rationed, and very little was allotted for pleasure driving; therefore, weddings were held close by and honeymoon trips were not far away.

We decided to be married at my parents' farm at 7:00 on a Saturday evening in June, with only our immediate families present for the ceremony. The reception, to which all our friends, relatives, and just about the entire community were invited, would be held following the wedding at 8:00 p.m.

We had both grown up on farms homesteaded in the 1850s by our early ancestors, in two adjacent small towns. Our parents had been friends since their high school days and now were pleased with plans to join the two families. They knew that many would come to help celebrate the big event.

My first year of teaching in another small town nearby had just ended, and Vaughn had only recently finished helping his dad plant a crop of potatoes. This seemed to be a good time to start our married life, so we set the date. We would initially be living in a small house which had been built years before on his father's farm for the hired help.

All future plans for our married life were clouded by the stark fact that men were being drafted daily to go to fight the war; our country was fighting on two fronts, in Japan and in Germany. Although farmers could be exempt because of the need to raise food for the armies, my new husband had volunteered to train as a Cadet in the U.S. Air Force. He had qualified for the training and was waiting to be called. We knew very little about our immediate future together. I had signed a contract for another year of teaching, this time in the school near our new home. It was a rural school with eight grades and I would be able to walk to work and save gas. When Vaughn would leave for service to his country, I knew that I would want to be busy.

The evening of our wedding arrived. It had been overcast most of the day, and I was worried about rain. The words to an old song, "Happy the bride that the sun shines on today," ran through my head, as I worked helping my mother prepare for the event. A neighbor came by to leave a gift and said, "Don't worry about the weather. The sun will be shining by evening." Happily she was right, and at suppertime the sun came out.

We had pictures taken before the ceremony on our lawn, with lots of sunshine to make them sharp and clear. I wore a navy silk suit with a frilly white blouse. My only sister Glenice, was my maid of honor, and wore a light two-piece dress with a dotted yoke. We felt beautiful, although quite unaccustomed to the corsages we wore. As Vaughn's only brother Merle, was serving in the air force overseas, a good friend, Beryl Kenney, agreed to be best man. They were both dressed in suits with white shirts and ties. The snapshots show us to be very happy, but gravely aware of the earnestness and wonder of the event. Being married then was for life, and we knew the seriousness of the vows we were about to make.

We stood before the minister in Mom's parlor, a pretty room abundantly decorated with summer flowers and looking festive. Our families sat around in their best finery and listened solemnly as we answered the minister's questions, affirming our vows. They were happy to be a part of this Service of Holy Matrimony and happy for us to be embarking on this new phase of our lives. We exchanged rings and before we realized, it was over; the minister announced that we were man and wife.

We kissed, then lots of hugs, congratulations and well wishes from family. We milled around to talk with everyone until the formal reception time, and other guests began to arrive. We were happy to see the huge crowd who had come to wish us well. The receiving line formed, and guests began passing through, some hugging, some teasing us about kissing the bride or hugging the groom. All were happy for us, and glad to be there to show it. Our cheeks and jaws were soon tired and lame from smiling and making small talk for so long. When the end of the line appeared, and all the guests were ready to be served the wedding cake and home-made ice cream, we strolled out on the lawn to get a breath of air. An uncle whispered to us to get away before the young men could decorate our car or cause a delay. So without a good-bye, or even a word to our parents, we slipped out to a shed where we had left the car hidden, jumped in and drove out the back way to escape the crowd. We were finally and actually married! Off to Portage Lake for a short honeymoon and together for the rest of our lives.

That was seventy-three years ago! We both say today that we can't believe so many years have gone by. I guess it is true: Time passes too fast when we're having fun.

Old Marital Problems
by Leonard Hutchins

This incident happened thirty-odd years ago. All the same, I had been married long enough to know better. It was a matter of knowing, or not knowing in this case, when to keep my mouth shut. Does that sound familiar?

My wife and I were reconditioning our recently-purchased, 1903-vintage, three-story, Oxbow hunting lodge. My first mistake (in this case) , was to announce that I was going to clean the chimney. I should have just done it. My wife explained that I should use a small burlap bag of quite round rocks, so the rocks would roll over one another and not get caught in the confined space. Her father said so.

I explained that the old chimney was bigger than two feet square, inside dimensions, and I was going to use a one-foot bag of bricks. The straight edge of the bricks would scrape the soot better. She said I was going to get into trouble, and I reminded her that a one-foot bag of bricks just couldn't get caught in a two-foot chimney. I'll give myself this much credit: I knew enough not to use the phrase, "silly woman."

By now you know where this story is headed. The bag of bricks, tied with a long rope, did as planned down through the attic, the third floor, the second floor, and halfway down the first floor. It was too dark down there for me to see how in the world a one-foot bag of bricks got stuck in a two-foot chimney. I tied the rope off to the chimney.

My wife had returned from her morning post-office and neighbor-visiting trip and was cooking in the kitchen when I went after a flashlight. I said nothing. The light showed what I had forgotten. The rear wall of the living room fireplace was built halfway into the chimney. The remaining space . . . well, you can see the whole thing.

As soon as I saw the problem, I knew how to solve it. A few years before, I had used army-surplus, armor-piercing bullets to penetrate a rock wall for a well pipe. Incidentally that rock wall was in a remote location and I took necessary precautions. I still had a few of those cartridges. However, my wife was in the kitchen so I couldn't safely shoot down the chimney.

Once again, I didn't keep my mouth shut when I should have. I didn't think ahead. It's all the same. If I had waited until the next morning, my wife would have gone after the mail as usual. I could have whacked the bricks, retrieved the bag, and nobody would have been the wiser.

Instead, I asked my wife, "Are you going to visit the neighbors this morning?"

She looked at me with suspicion. "I just came back," she said.

My brain didn't engage. "Why don't you go visit someone else?" I asked.

"You got those bricks caught in the chimney, didn't you?" she said.

Anyway she left for another visit. The rifle did as expected. So far as I know, no bullet escaped the chimney, and life went on.

However. Even today, my wife wins an occasional argument by asking, "Are you going to use bricks to clean the chimney again?"

WE OTHER VETERANS
by Phyllis Hutchins

I feel like a veteran because I accompanied my husband, Leonard, during sixteen months of active military service at Camp Polk, Louisiana. Things were different there. *Really.*

They had what they called a "free range" law. The animals had free run of the place unless you fenced them out of your piece of the military housing complex. So we fenced off a little front lawn play area for our little son Peter.

This worked okay until one day I looked out the back window. A huge horse was eating grass under my clothes line—with a pair of my clean sheets draped over its back. The big miserable thing paid me no heed even when I went out and told it what I thought of it. So we fenced off my clothes line space and I washed the sheets again.

Our housing units were built on concrete posts of varying lengths to compensate for uneven ground. That left part of the underside of the house open and part closed in. A huge boar pig learned to corner huge sow pigs under our house to make love. I didn't need that many sleepless nights so we fenced off their recreation area.

But I'll tell you what. It didn't take me long to learn that snakes, big or little, wanted no part of my broom.

It was just the animals. The Louisiana friends we made were great.

LUCKY WIN

by Leonard Hutchins

Lucky wins make life interesting. An out-of-the-baseball-park, four run, home run; a hole-in-one golf shot; a ringer in a horseshoe game; two deer with one shot; shooting a glass bottle rim from a skunk in trouble—all memorable. The skunk shot was mine some fifty years ago.

One day, wife, Phyllis, decided to accompany me to hunt a few partridges in the upper Aroostook River watershed. She even packed a picnic lunch. Things went well—we had two birds—until I drove through an abandoned logging camp yard.

"Leonard," Phyllis said, "Stop. There is a beautiful, cute little skunk. I just love skunks. Their black and white fur is just so, so beautiful." I had my fill of skunks many years before. But I stopped. If seeing a skunk at a distance makes her day, why not? "Oh," Phyllis said, "there is something wrong with that beautiful, lovely, little creature. Look, Leonard. What's that?"

Sure enough there was a skunk, and there was something wrong. "That is the neck of a quart canning jar around the skunk's neck. Your little friend must have stuck his head into a jar on the camp dump," I said.

"Leonard," Phyllis said, "go pull that awful glass ring from that dear, little creature's neck." Like I said, I'd had my fill of skunks many years before.

"Look Phyllis," I said, "why don't I shoot that glass ring off your skunk's neck? That way I can stay out of the skunk's range and you won't have to sleep with a skunky husband."

"Leonard," Phyllis said, "don't you shoot that beautiful animal."

"No problem," I assured her as I stepped out of the pickup and slid a magazine into my pistol.

"Leonard," Phyllis said, "if you shoot that splendid creature, I'm going to cook it and you're going to eat it."

Hey just what I needed to calm my nerves as I lined up my pistol sights on the very top of the skunk's glass collar. "Would she really cook that skunk?" I wondered. Well, maybe. She thinks for herself.

CRACK, went my pistol. Anxiously I looked for the skunk. Will wonders never cease! There in the camp yard was the broken glass ring. The freed skunk scurried under the camp.

THE WHITE GOOSE
by Leonard Hutchins

This event should not have happened. Not to me anyway. I had only the bird's best interest in mind.

Late in a fall migrating season, a beautiful white goose appeared on a small pond near several Oxbow homes. We neighbors assumed our splendid visitor would rest for a day or so, and join a flock flying south. Not so. Day after day passed and ice formed around the edge of the pond. Our visitor, we thought would have to fly soon, or be accessible to wild animals or two dogs which lived nearby.

One day I looked down the road and could hardly believe my eyes. Our new feathered neighbor had walked by the two homes with dogs and was nearly to our place.

Snap decision: The goose can't fly. Catch it before the fox does. Make a pen for our kids' new pet.

Splendid idea. I readied myself with a sturdy fruit basket, and waited in the road. Wary, the goose kept coming. I lunged, ended up in a soggy ditch, and the nervous bird flew away over a field, across acres of woodland, and over a ridge headed south.

Only then did I realize that my wife and a neighbor were laughing at me.

And they still do.

THE WONDERS OF SPRING!
by Norma Ouellette

When the snow has been around for a while and people are tired of the cold, "When will spring be here?" is often heard. It is a wonder, when the leaves are peeking out on the tree limbs and the daffodils, tulips, forsythia and lily of the valley show. And then we will see the fiddleheads! I started picking fiddleheads when I was quite young. My mother and my aunts would go out on the Presque Isle Road near the river. Everyone had a favorite spot.

I continued picking as long as I lived in the area. Then when my husband was in the military we moved to so many states and of course no fiddleheads. His last assignment was in New Hampshire. I asked about fiddleheads but didn't get any answers until my sister-in-law was down to visit and introduced us to Linda and Carl Wheeler. My sister-in-law, Joanne and Linda were neighbors in Fort Kent. Carl and Linda were the ones who gave us a trip where fiddleheads grew.

What a gift that was! We picked in the same spot on the Souhegan River. We were in Milford, New Hampshire for years. During that time, the many people we met there had been born up here in the County. One or two couples from Connecticut drove up to pick. They were also from the County. I thought we had met them all.

An elderly gentleman approached us one time asking where we came from. I said Bedford, which is the town we were living in.

He said, "No, where did you come from originally?" I said, "Caribou."

He then said, "I knew it! I'm from Mars Hill!"

Oxbow Lodge: A View from the Kitchen
by Phyllis Hutchins, the cook

On April 13, 1968, my 40th birthday, what a present I received! It was 50 feet square and three stories high with 12 rooms. My family and I moved into Oxbow Lodge.

Built in 1903 by guide and trapper Will Atkins, the lodge housed Will's sportsmen, hunters and fishermen, as they traveled in wagons between the Masardis Bangor and Aroostook train station and the back country sportsman's paradise west of Oxbow. My husband, Leonard, and I were proud. We felt we were part of Aroostook sporting history.

However, my birthday present showed its 65 years of use—foundation, kitchen, plumbing, guest rooms, dining room—you name it—everything needed something. Leonard, in his spare time from teaching at Ashland Community High School, and our oldest son, Peter, started shoring up the crumbling foundation. I supervised putting my kitchen (my world) in order—new stoves, refrigerators, sinks, cupboards, closets. Happy. Happy. Happy. We didn't have time to wonder if we needed our heads examined.

I think my friend and neighbor, Kathleen Currier, preserved my sanity. She had worked many years in back-country sporting camps.

I could cook, but she knew what else I was supposed to know. She agreed to work as needed to spiff up the old place and get me started.

"Oh, well," we thought, "school summer vacation is coming. We won't have guests to interfere with getting our place ready for fall deer hunters." But during our first week in my birthday present, a United States Forest Service officer stopped by looking for a place for his crew.

"Sorry," I said as he warmed his hands over my old kitchen wood-fired cook stove. "We just moved in. The old furnace isn't safe to use."

"Hey, look," he said, "this stove works. We're living in tents now."

Instant problems. We didn't have beds enough, and I wondered how our four kids, ages 10 to 16, and our new guests would get along. Leonard took time enough from the foundation job to make a dozen or so bed frames. Our kids got along so well with our guests that I had to lay down some rules to keep the kids out of the guests' rooms. Some problems didn't happen.

However, some problems, or blessings—depending on one's point of view—I never imagined. Leonard was coaching the Ashland Community High School cross-country team, and the kids decided that Oxbow Lodge was a good place for a pizza party. A pizza party in a hunting lodge? Incredible.

Well, the USFS crew had moved on. My family rattled around in the old place like a half dozen peas in a big shoebox. The place had, for sure, never experienced that many kids. Why not try it?

It was a blessing for sure. Noisy. Energetic. Laughing. Accompanying parents carried pizzas from kitchen to crowded dining and living rooms. One fellow said, "I think I'd be more successful trying to feed a heard of hogs than that bunch." That was the first of many great pizza parties.

As delightful as the party was, it showed us an unanticipated problem. We needed a fire escape. The solution was apparent. Build a set of steps in the three-story front porch. Since the old porch was too decayed to be safe, we needed to take it down, roof first then each floor at a time to make room for the new structure. Understandable. The foundation job stretched into the summer, and material for the new fire escape piled up.

I had no reason to suspect trouble, not even one day when Leonard asked me to keep the kids away from the front of the building—which I did—thankfully.

Suddenly a ripping, tearing, thunderous, building-quaking roar terrified me back in my kitchen. I was sure the front wall had fallen out of Oxbow Lodge. I screamed for the kids, and they all answered from upstairs, wanting to know what had happened. I hurried to the front door. There was the porch roof lying on the porch deck, right in front of the front door. There was Leonard, untying a rope, one end from the car and the other end from a porch post.

I regret what I screamed at Leonard that day, but I haven't apologized yet. However, it took a surprisingly short time for Leonard and Peter to remove the old porch and frame the new one up including the new fire escape.

One Sunday afternoon, one of our neighbors, an excellent Maine guide, brought two "sports" from New York to stay for a week. Those fellows really wanted a bear to take home. No problem. The guide knew the bear better than the bear did. Early Monday morning they hung their bear on our new front porch. Our guests had the week to fish, and they were delighted.

Now, even fresh, a bear doesn't smell all that great, and it was a hot week. By Wednesday Leonard and Peter had to do work around the back where it smelled better. I locked the front door. That Saturday morning I couldn't believe my eyes. Our New York guests, happy and proud, loaded that bear into their panel truck—with the windows closed—and started to New York. I was becoming used to unexpected events.

Very unexpected indeed. Friends called asking us to change our hunting lodge to a dining room. "Wait. Wait. Wait." I thought. "How many people will drive all the way to Oxbow for a meal? How much to cook. Can I do that and keep hunting and fishing guests? How will I know if I don't try? After all, the kids' pizza party turned out okay."

My neighbor, Rita Sherman, and her daughters, Susan, Sheila, and Sharon, joined my daughters, Dorothy and Susan, urging me to go for it. With that backing I advertised, cooked up a storm—and hoped. During the first week of cooking preparations, my nerves frayed. Also Leonard's maintenance work required new shingles on the roof—three stories above the very hard ground. Just talk about frayed nerves.

One very warm morning, out of the corner of my eye, I saw something green drop down by my kitchen window. *GREEN*! Leonard was wearing a green jacket that day. My nerves detonated. I screamed. I ran outdoors screaming. There was the green jacket lying on the lawn—safe, sound, and empty.

"Hey," Leonard yelled down to me from the roof, "What happened? What are you yelling about, anyway?

If I'd been up there on the roof, I'd have thrown him off. But anyway, he didn't throw his coat down again.

In due time, and to my great relief, Leonard finished shingling the roof.

However, Leonard and the roof, a smelly bear, and the front porch weren't my only concerns. For the restaurant effort I cooked up a storm, and, alas, very few people came to dinner. At least the neighbors liked the leftovers.

So, should I give up the restaurant idea? After all, Oxbow was a long way to drive just for a meal. My crew, my friends, neighbors, and daughters, guessed not. We decided to have a smorgasbord Sundays and serve by reservation only the rest of the week. That way, I had to guess how much to cook only one day a week.

Those days, those weeks, were enlightening. For instance, running out of ingredients a few times taught me to organize. (Oxbow is a long way from the grocery store.) I kept a clipboard for meal planning, and one for cooking needs, and I kept them both ahead for the next week.

I soon developed a sixth sense for estimating how many guests would come to a Sunday smorgasbord. Some events, the Northern Maine Fair and the Potato Blossom Festival for instance, reduced my trade. The weather, a nice sunny afternoon for instance, increased my trade.

And I soon learned that children, delightful anyway, were also a big attraction. I kept an assortment of homemade cookies for my most welcome guests to have after dinner, and to take home for friends. Young parents said the kids often decided to go to the "cookie place" for the Sunday outing.

When our leaves turned to fall shades (earlier here in Aroostook than farther south) I received calls from our second-childhood children, senior citizens. (Since I'm one of them now I can write about us.) Groups from churches, nursing homes and clubs in the Bangor area made reservations and came by busloads. And I had worried that people wouldn't drive from local communities to Oxbow for a meal! They too were delighted to select from the cookie assortment to take home for their shut-in friends.

However, my "sixth sense" didn't always work precisely during fall leaf season. My sister visited one fall Sunday. She watched us set up a smorgasbord for ten dozen or so guests. At eleven o'clock she looked worried. "What will we do with all this leftover food?" she wondered. We smiled. At twelve o'clock or so the road was lined with cars, and there was a line through the front porch and into the dining room. We watched the "How can this happen?" expression on her face. Soon she cut herself a piece of pumpkin pie, her favorite, our mother's recipe, and since she hadn't had a piece in a long, long time, she squirreled it away in a cupboard. As luck would have it, one of the dining room girls needed one more piece of pie for her last party. She had no idea why it was tucked away, but there it was—just what she needed. I made my sister another pie.

Before leaf season turned to hunting season we advertised ahead so our dining room guests wouldn't drive to Oxbow to find a closed dining room. Single hunters and parties of six or eight, mostly from Massachusetts south to Pennsylvania, made reservations—usually for a week. By and large they were a friendly, good-natured, generous bunch. Our kids learned more about hunting than most kids do. Tip money was saved in a "tip jar" and divided among the help at season's end—just in time to buy Christmas presents.

For me, the best part of hunting seasons were the endless variety of events—mostly funny...

A young hunter said to Kay, "I try to keep the closet door in my room closed, but every morning it's wide open. Does that happen all the time?"

Kay, a usually truthful, innocent looking lady, has an odd sense of humor. She explained, "Mrs. Atkins, the first, first lady of Oxbow Lodge, stays in that closet. She comes out every night to see that her Oxbow Lodge is kept neat and clean. I am very careful to please Mrs. Atkins."

Next morning Kay called down to me in the kitchen from the young fellow's room, "Come up here. You've got to see this." The young fellow had jammed his bed against the closet door, apparently to keep Mrs. Atkins in her place. He didn't return to Oxbow Lodge for future hunting seasons.

A hunter stood talking to me in the kitchen. His high-school-aged son walked in, all smiles, carrying a goose. Dad, son, and goose disappeared out the door. Dad and son returned in time for supper.

"Sorry," the youngster said to me. "I didn't know I wasn't supposed to shoot a goose. I hope I don't get you in trouble."

"Goose?" I asked. "What goose? You better hurry or someone will eat your supper."

One of our hunters returned to the lodge one afternoon, his head and hands cut, scratched, bloody. Gruesome. Really.

"A bobcat got you?" I asked as I helped with his wounds.

"I don't like your owls," the fellow said. "It kept attacking me until I got back to my pickup. I'm not going to wear my parka with a fur-trimmed hood anymore."

Toward the end of the hunting season there were often a dozen or two dozen deer hanging in the garage. People stopped to take pictures. A young hunter shot a particularly handsome buck one year. He was proud. Many people, natives and "from away," took his picture with his deer. On the Sunday morning his party was to leave Oxbow Lodge the beautiful buck was gone—stolen. A window was wedged open. There were tracks. The young fellow was left with only pictures of his trophy. I felt ugly and very sorry for our young hunter.

Game wardens don't get much sleep during hunting season. They always have fish and game poachers to deal with, but in hunting season they also have to deal with inexperienced hunters who sometimes get lost. Leonard sometimes went with a warden to find a lost hunter. My 4:00 a.m. to 10:00 p.m. days didn't leave me much sleep time either, but when a search party was out I kept the kitchen open.

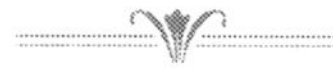

In 1977 I was still young enough to want a bigger dining room. (Leonard said I'd lost my marbles.) The foundation works didn't take long. The framework and the roof really went great. However, fitting two-and-a-half-inch flooring into a 50-foot x 50-foot floor was something else. I felt sorry for Leonard—sort of. But when it was all done we were both happy, and I had room for a lot of repeat customers, especially little ones.

But only for several years. At first my body clock went awry now and then. But eventually it was constant. In 1985 we sold Oxbow Lodge—well, sort of. We kept our memories, our friends, our dreams, and the old place was still there for us to enjoy when we drove by… until December 2013 when the Oxbow Lodge burned to the ground. We still have our memories, our friends, our dreams.

Note: Phyllis and Leonard Hutchins owned and operated the Oxbow Lodge for eighteen years—a remarkable feat for a remarkable family.

New Generations

Join the March

Thoreau and I

by Marilyn Hoyt Sprague Chase

Some of us believe everything we hear. Others of us, everything we see. And a particular breed, of which I'm one, believes everything we read. I am putty in the hands of the author, the poet, the crusader. Everything from Chesterton to cookbook becomes a way of life if I can fit it to myself. I embrace it. I live it. I expound it. And sometimes I regret it.

The first time that I read Thoreau's *Walden*, I was captive. There was no turning back. No simple closing of the book. I, too, had to find a Walden. Because I, too, wished to "live deliberately, to front only the essential facts of life, and see if I could not learn what it had to teach." Was I not one of the mass of women who lead lives of discontent, "idly complaining of the hardness of their lot or of the times?" I was.

The not-so-quiet cause of most of my quiet desperation, (Jonathan, age eight; Christopher, seven; Susan, five; and Robin, one) had to go with me. I argued that if Thoreau had had children, he would have taken them to Walden Pond. He never would have reared his children in a town. Did he not write, "better if they had been born in the open pasture and suckled by a wolf?"

The time was around the first of May but already the weather was hot and humid, and the streets were full of dust from the seemingly endless road construction. Outside on our shadeless lawn, the children wandered aimlessly around. The sandbox had lost its appeal and so had the swings. There wasn't a breath of fresh air anywhere—only dust.

"Look at them," I would complain to anyone and everyone. "They look like prisoners in a compound."

I had no money to spend for lake vacations. I had to find a Walden that would be rent-free. But where? The children have a great-uncle,

Dr. Raymond Pendleton, who had a summer home on Islesboro Island off the coast of Maine. (He has since retired and the summer home has become his winter home as well.) About a quarter of a mile in back of this house is an old log cabin which had been built on the cliffs overlooking East Penobscot Bay.

I wrote the uncle that very day. Kind man that he is, he answered, "Yes, I would love to let you have it. Come early and stay late."

Economy

I announced my plans. All my friends and relatives (except the uncle) immediately tried to talk me out of them. It wasn't safe for the children. It was too isolated and the uncle was only there during August. In the meantime, I would be without a car, almost a mile from my nearest neighbor. There was no electricity, no telephone, no bathroom.

Determined, I stretched my budget to buy essentials—bedrolls, army cots, camp stove, lantern. Someone loaned me a camp refrigerator. My special luxuries were a field guide to rocks and minerals, a book about trees, one about flowers, another on birds, and of course *Walden*.

On my last day at home, I began to have qualms and started debating with myself.

Probably the cabin's well is caved-in. I'll have to carry water down from Uncle Ray's house.

I'm strong, I can do it.

The path to the cabin is probably grown over with alders.

I can cut the alders down.

I'll have to watch the children every minute. Those high cliffs are dangerous. It won't be like having them safely inside a fenced-in yard. And they could get lost in the woods.

Don't worry, I plan to watch them.

The first day of July, we started. The children had excitedly assembled their own camping equipment: Boy Scout knives and hatchets, a magnifying glass, a favorite doll, and bows and arrows. Even though I had my own private doubts about the expedition, when I strapped my sheath knife to my belt and waved goodbye to my neighbors (who'd given me no more than a week in the woods), I felt quite as adventurous as one starting a first African safari.

Where I lived and What I Lived for

The pasture was out. So was the wolf, but I had found my Walden. It was larger than Thoreau's pond, but it was the perfect spot to "dispel the clouds" which hung over my own brow, and to "pluck the finer fruits of life."

The cabin did not look as if it had appeared out of a storybook. There were only two rooms divided by a huge gray stone fireplace. The kitchen had a black iron stove and an iron sink which didn't drain, but from its front window was one of the most beautiful views in the world. There was an island in the sunlight, another in the shadow, and yet another enshrouded in bluish fog. Then nothing but the mist, the open Atlantic, and the ghost of Thoreau.

Housewarming

With the first morning I began to suspect that a lot of "factitious and superfluously coarse labors of life" were going to hinder my elevation. Water? I had to walk fifty yards to the crumbling stone well and draw it out. This involved a lot of motion and conversation as I frantically held on to dirty little feet, while everyone took turns peering down the shallow hole.

"It looks dirty and scary down there."

"Look at all those little wiggly fish."

"Those aren't fish, dumbhead. Those are germs."

"Be careful!" I grabbed Susan by her pajama bottoms. "You'll fall in."

I found a long stick with a hooked end, put it under the handle of the pail, laid flat on my stomach and lowered it into the water.

Halfway down the well, it occurred to me that one of these mornings, they might become motherless.

"If I fall in, what would you do?" I yelled.

"Push you the rest of the way?" Christopher asked in his that-would-be-a-fun-thing-to-do tone of voice.

I've wondered since, if I'm the only mother in history who has had to teach her children to push her down the well. The depth was shallow, only three feet, but the opening was so small that I would have needed a good shove to get my feet down and turned around.

Breakfast was an even more hysterical meal in the woods than in town. The best I could manage on the little portable gas stove was usually over-cooked sausages and scorched eggs that tasted the way a wet dog smells.

After we ate, I waded around on spilled orange juice and scrambled eggs trying to find four shirts, shorts and toothbrushes. It was noon by the time we were dressed, dishes done, bedrolls airing or drying in the big pine tree whose lower, dead branches served as my clothesline. Then we had to walk to a general store, a mile away, to buy bread and meat, and "take up a little life into our pores."

Higher Laws

We walked up through the alder swamp, picking up all the toads in the path and putting them in our pockets. We stopped, and discussed at length, each fascinating pile of animal excrement left there the night before. We stuck our feet in the black anthill. We stuck our feet in the red anthill. We found a turtle and put it into the grocery basket.

Finally we trooped down and into the store, not leaving a bottle or can untouched, and insisting that if we couldn't have another bottle of pop, we just wouldn't "go back to that old log cabin home." Unlike Thoreau, my children will never have to repent of their good behavior.

We started back. I not only had to carry most of the groceries, but Robin, too. We returned the turtle. We stuck our feet in the red ant hill. We stuck our feet in the black ant hill. We did this every day for two months and two days.

Solitude

We spent most of our afternoons in the outhouse. I was no sooner happily ensconced on the beach, when "Mom, I have to go to the bathroom!"

"Well, just go up and go."

"No, I'm afraid."

"Oh, Jon, there is nothing to be afraid of."

"I'm afraid I'll fall through that hole."

It wasn't safe to leave the other three alone on the shore. All five of us had to trudge up the cliffs to the "bathroom."

It was quite fancy as outhouses go. Some gregarious architect had designed it with two holes. An obvious convenience, as I pointed out to the children.

"This is why the man built it this way," I would reason patiently with Christopher. "So you could go with Jon, and Mom could sit in the sun."

"But the man didn't build me, did he? I don't want to and I won't!!"

We climbed the cliffs to the bathroom all afternoon, every afternoon for two months and two days. Thus I was enabled to apprehend what was "sublime and noble only by the perpetual instilling and drenching of the reality" which surrounded me.

Sounds

With the first week, the children became tanned, healthier and dirtier than they'd ever been before. We explored. Down and over the shore from us were numerous beaches. We named them: Jonathan's Beach, Christopher's Beach, Susan's Beach, and Robin's Beach. After every tide, we scavenged. Bits of colored glass—water-worn smooth, fossil rocks, and if you used your imagination, Indian messages on sheets of birch bark. One of their most cherished treasures was a sand-filled plum-colored sock which they firmly believed belonged to some poor soul who was shipwrecked on one of the outlying islands.

There were banks of clay to make bowls, ashtrays, maps, or just to throw at each other. We built, wrote and played in the sand, using some to make sand pictures with paper and glue on rainy days and some to pour on each other's heads on sunny days. Robin, the baby, spent endless hours collecting shells and stringing them later.

Even the rainy days were different. The boys could literally climb the cabin walls, which they did at regular intervals. We would spend an afternoon with scissors and construction paper, staging little puppet shows, amid arguing, fussing and having tantrums. Sometimes they'd sit in front of an open fire munching popcorn, but spilling more, while I read to them—anything that they'd listen to.

Reading

Needless to say, I anticipated the sunset more than the dawn. After the last child was zippered into his sleeping bag, I'd flop in one chair, prop my feet and gas lantern on another, and read for hours. Slightly trashy novels in which everyone was corrupted by wealth and easy living appealed to me most. I didn't follow Thoreau's dictum to read on mental "tip-toe."

I obtained these books at the local library, which wasn't far from the store. We walked there every Wednesday afternoon, watched the puppet shows and loaded up on comic books. The children didn't want to read on mental tip-toe either.

Brute Neighbors

I never really learned to anticipate nature, particularly her mice. They were all over the place—in the cupboards, in the bedrolls on chilly mornings, even in the oven of the old cookstove. Unlike fictional mice, these weren't scared by a "Boo!" or a "Scat!" I had to push them bodily back through the holes in the chinking, all the while with Jon reminding me unctuously that, after all, they were "just God's little creatures."

Remember that old game? I see something—it's round and green, or whatever shape and color it is.

"I see something," said Susan, early one morning as we were lying in our cots looking out the curtainless windows. "I see something and it's round and plump!"

"Is it the milk bottle?"

"No."

"Is it the pillow?"

"No."

"I give up. Go back to sleep."

"It's a man!" She shrieked, pointing. So it was. Round and Plump was peering in at us looking as surprised as I felt.

A friend had loaned me a shotgun before I left civilization behind. "Now you have a perfect right to defend yourself against anyone who bothers you," he solemnly assured me.

Defend myself? Round and Plump was my very first visitor and I was so delighted to see him, I could have kissed him.

"Come in! Come in! We're just getting breakfast." I called. The Emperor in his new clothes didn't have much less on then I in my shorty pajamas, but I pulled on a sweater and slacks as he was making his way to the back door.

"Didn't know that there was anybody here," he drawled. "I live on the other side of the Island. Just thought I'd stroll down and look around."

He stayed for breakfast and several cups of coffee. As he was leaving, he said with startling candor, "When I was younger, I wasn't too right in the head, either. But I outgrew it. Maybe you will too."

Visitors

My "pumpkin" started to become crowded. After Round and Plump's visit, we had people almost every day. Frequent strollers on our beach was a honeymoon couple, who obviously preferred their own company. This didn't bother my children who tagged along behind them, using me as interpreter for endless shouted questions.

"Mom, ask them if they like snakes."

"Mom, asked them if they like onions."

"Mom, ask them if they like Playtex bras."

Once some red-faced, panting fathers with their more physically-fit sons, climbed into view after an arduous hike over the rocks. With Motherearth style, I offered them a drink from the well.

The drama was going splendidly until my gracious passing of the cool dipper to a parched father was intercepted by Jon, who snatched it and drank it down greedily, thirstily, and firstly.

After that I didn't pretend to be anything else but some sort of nut with four unmanageable children.

We had visitors from New York City who stayed a week. When the going was rough, such as three rainy days in succession, they would converse in German. I'm sure it wasn't a discussion of Thoreau, either.

We ate mussels with them and wild mushrooms. Just as I was serving them for the first time, my mushroom expert warned, "Better not give any to the children, just in case... ."

It was less than an hour later that I doubled with pain. I turned to my visitor who at least had the grace to look somewhat abashed.

"I thought you said that you knew all about mushrooms!" I groaned.

"The book said that they were hard to digest," he admitted in weak defense.

Whether it was the mushrooms or the mussels which had been full of little pearls, I don't know. I survived and have continued eating them with no further difficulty.

My sister (also from the City) visited us, with her husband, two children, and ten pieces of luggage.

After her first startled glance around and horrified, "Marilyn, these children will either get lost in the woods or kill themselves on the cliffs," she went into the cabin and stayed there during her entire four-day visit. She annoyed me immensely by doing her laundry in my dishpan and stalking my mice with an axe.

The idea of using the shotgun on some of my visitors began to appeal to me. I would rather be "crowded on a velvet cushion" then be driven mad on a pumpkin.

Former Inhabitants

One afternoon after a heavy thunder shower, the children hurried out, eager to play in their little "rivers" running down the banks to the shore. "Mom, Mom," I heard them calling. "Come see!"

I ran out. It was late afternoon and the rain and sun had made a perfect rainbow across the sky, ending in the water just in front of us.

"Look Mom! The rainbow ends here!" exclaimed Susan with wonder. "Did you know that we were living at the end of the rainbow?"

I winked at the Ghost's smug expression. "You may as well go away and haunt someone else," I exorcised. "We have even exceeded you."

Conclusion

Long ago, I lost my long fingernails, my complexion, and my copy of Thoreau's *Walden* which fell in the Bay that first summer. Since then we have been back to our Walden for several summers, and the children have grown into ardent disciples of Thoreau.

And I? Since age "has not profited so much as it has lost," I'll always be regretting that I'm "not as wise as the day I was born," or at least before I learned to read.

Memorable Kid Moments

by Leonard and Phyllis Hutchins

Some events happen right then, and some accumulate in steps.

Step one: Son, Peter, and friends went hunting near our woods camp and nearby outhouse.

Step two: He felt the urge, stepped into the facility, closed the door, and stood his shotgun in the corner.

Step three: He doesn't like spiders. There, up in the corner was a big spider.

Step four: He decided that ridding the world of that spider was worth a shotgun shell.

Step five (A): WHAM. The charge of shot embedded the spider into the outhouse wall.

Step five (B): The blast in that confined space deafened Peter for a short while.

Step six: Peter's hearing gradually returned, and he realized that his friends outside were trying to decide if he had an accident, committed suicide, or what. At any rate, they were too chicken to open the outhouse door. What a great opportunity to keep his friends in suspense!

Step seven: However, Peter soon realized that sitting in an outhouse isn't the greatest place to pull a prank on your friends.

Step eight: Peter chickened out first. He opened the outhouse door.

∼∼∼

Son, Paul had early trouble with clocks and time. "Paul," his mother explained, "the short hand tells you what hour it is in the morning or the afternoon. The long hand tells you what minute it is in the hour.

"Oh," Paul said, "I know all that. What is confusing me is that third little hand that keeps whizzing around in there." It took mother a while, but she taught Paul to tell time—right to the second.

∽∽∽

Years later, in our local community college, Paul had much better luck with a project—making a kite that would fly, and flying it. He bought extra twine just in case his project really worked.

It did, indeed, fly—extra twine and all. The local airport was close to the community college. The community college received an urgent telephone call. The airport people wondered if the community college people had any idea what was showing up on the airport radar.

The Great Carrot Pull
by Joan Allen

When Vaughn and I sold our house on Barton Street we had a house built at Hanson Lake in Mapleton on the lake side. We had always loved being at camp at Shin Pond on weekends and vacations, having access to boats, fish, loons and other amenities that come with nature and serenity.

In the course of smoothing out the big land around the house, we had a garden plot dug with the extra. We thought of keeping some of our own vegetables in a cold cellar room in the corner of our basement. Vaughn, the erstwhile farmer, enjoyed planting and cultivating the plot and growing peas, carrots, lettuce, etc. We found we could "winter" the carrots best in the cold cellar.

By the time we had our first two grandchildren, Lindsay and Derrick, and they became interested in the garden, we thought we could include them in the harvesting of the carrots, so we dreamed up The Great Carrot Pull for them to come pull all the carrots up.

Once told it was time for The Great Carrot Pull, they couldn't wait to come out and get started pulling them up. We put the carrots in baskets and put them in the cellar.

The kids were happy and dirty and we all had a great time. We *all* loved that day!

To Dory, Our "Favorite Oldest" Grandchild
by Maxine Smith

"Gram, May I have the trash in the sewing room?" you asked.
"I'm making something pretty for you."
So, rummaging around you found pieces of lace,
Some yarn and scraps of bright cloth to paste;
Making a valentine for me to treasure
From my first-born grandchild.

"Gram, Could I please come live with you?" you begged.
I smiled, and hugged, telling you how sad your folks would be.
You cuddled closer, teasing, "But they could come to see me.
And sometimes stay to eat, and visit, and play with me."
All the while those big brown eyes fixed on me—Trying to
        wear me down, and gaining ground.

"May we all come to sleep over?" you asked.
"We want to learn to knit, Gram. Will you show us today?"
So we searched out pretty yarn, and needles for three to learn;
After mile of knotted yarn, and hundreds of stitches dropped,
You each did knit a long bright scarf for a Cabbage Patch kid:
Three little granddaughters learning to knit and purl.

From the high school: "Gram, can you come for me around
        three?

I have play practice tonight, and need to stay down."
So, we had a short but precious time to visit before supper,
I, reading aloud from the playbook; you, memorizing your
    lines.
You learned swiftly, and we each had fun acting the parts.
Then, too soon, time was up and you had to go.

"Will you bring Leigh when you come to Bangor?" you begged.
"I miss everyone so much since I've been here at Orono."
So your brother went with us, and stayed with you on campus;
Hectic weekend night at your dorm, with more than one
    fire alarm,
Yet, you were happier the day we left, and we felt better, too.
Homesick isn't easy, even for grandparents.

"I hate to go down on the coast alone," you spoke tearfully.
"Dad says I must, I have to have a job. I'd rather stay here."
My heart ached. Horror stories about young girls living alone
Filled my mind; haunting me throughout that sleepless night.
Soon, word came back: Two cousins met you there in Bar
    Harbor;
Three college girls, blessed and happy with exciting
    summer jobs.

Grandchildren are a special, wonderfully precious, part of life.
Then we know how blessed we are, to have this second chance.
When heartstrings join our lives for such a short, sweet, while;
And happy memories are born; a long, long line of love is
    drawn
To tie you close even when you're far away. That line is strong,
And you will always know that you can follow it and hang
    on tight.

—Gram Smith
March 23, 1996

GRANDSONS
by Phyllis and Leonard Hutchins

Alan, at age about six years, acquired a piece of high-class elastic perhaps eight feet long. One morning he tied one end to the stairs railing and the other end around his bare chest. He backed down the hall stretching the elastic.

"Don't do that Al," his older brother, Michael advised—several times.

It was really good elastic. It stretched nicely across the bedroom.

"Al," Michael said, "you…"

Whack! Scream!

Mother bounded up the stairs. "Michael," she demanded, what did you do to Alan?"

It took a few frantic minutes to straighten that event out.

A PRIVILEGE
by Leonard Hutchins

The problem with writing about an Allagash River canoe trip is the limits of language. Bigger than life and old as time, The River always lives up to its world class billing. As a bonus for our 1994 trip, it offered a favorable pitch of water. Near Chamberlain Bridge, between Chamberlain and Telos Lakes, we were gratified to see the water invading normally dry grasses along the shore.

With enthusiastic support but not much help from our fifth companion, a big red dog—named Red, of course; two grandchildren, Michael and Alan Michaud; their father, Mark; and I packed two pickup loads of food and camping gear (what used to be called wangan) into two canoes. That delighted me, because my wife, who has an eye for such things, had said it couldn't be done. But 20-foot canoes are that big.

Because we had limited time off from work, Mark and I had decided to use a motor on one canoe so we could tow the other. Shoving off, we shouted assurances to my wife, Phyllis, and Mark's father, Lawrence, that we'd see them 90-odd miles downriver at Allagash village in five days.

Slipping under the steel bridge and up Chamberlain Thoroughfare, it seemed as if we had already gone centuries back in time. So many feelings were evoked at once, that it's hard to record them all.

First there was the deep pleasure at being part of such a three-generation adventure.

Then there was the satisfaction of finally seeing Chamberlain and Telos Lakes, whose water flow had been changed from north to south by a dam built on Chamberlain and the canal, the Telos Cut, dug from Telos to Webster Lake in 1841 to float logs from the area down the Penobscot River to Bangor. "Stealing" water was resented. Control was contested in courts and with fists—even with armed guards, it is said. In my mind, I saw the caulk-booted loggers working logs out of the bushes along the banks with peaveys and pick poles. I imagined a cumbersome side-wheel paddleboat pulling a raft of logs toward Telos Lake. I thought I'd like to show those old loggers one of the big diesel trucks that haul logs from that area today.

Finally, I felt a more pervasive presence. After all, the loggers' years on the Allagash were only a flash in the pan. Indians lived there for centuries, using only what they needed to sustain themselves. I found myself musing about what it would have been like to live, talk and learn with them.

"Hey!" Mark yelled from the rear canoe. "Don't get too close to that point!" My attention adjusted a few centuries and I moved the tiller.

The canoes skirted a shallow water point and we glided onto the broad expanse of Chamberlain Lake. A light breeze ruffled the immense gray-blue lake surface. Fleecy white clouds served as a backdrop for a sprinkling of tall pines dominating mixed hardwood and spruce-fir growth on low ridges around the lake. Ducks flying by, soaring ospreys, a few acrobatic seagulls and an occasional loon bobbing low in the rippled lake punctuated the solitude.

A white granite boulder, perhaps a canoe length wide and three canoe lengths long, protruded from the lake. It was a favorite with the gulls. I wondered if Indian children had played on it when the water was low. Several small islands with large trees looked from a distance like ships with green sails. Nugent's camps, an institution in the area, looked from mid-lake to be in postage-stamp-sized clearings.

"That's Chamberlain Farm," Michael said above the drone of the motor when we were about halfway up the 12-mile-long lake, pointing to a building and an unidentifiable large brown something.

During the late 1800s and early 1900s, the 600-acre farm supplied local loggers and their horses with food. We carefully beached the canoes, and I had a mixed experience. The building, used by the Allagash Wilderness Waterway rangers who operate the area, was fairly new. But the farm's barns, bunkhouse and cookrooms were gone. I felt a loss.

Then, I discovered after much study and mental reconstructing of rotted-away wooden parts that the "large brown something" on the shore was a rusting steam engine for a paddle-wheel boat. I also recognized bush-grown, rotting remnants of the boat itself. I felt like a tornado victim who has found a family heirloom in the wreckage of his home. Unfortunately, it was a few shades too heavy to take with me.

Similar experiences awaited a few miles farther up the lake, when we stopped to camp at Lock Dam. The original dams from 1841, a lock system used to lift logs a few feet from Eagle Lake to Chamberlain Lake, were gone. Only the contour of the location helped me imagine the structure.

The present dam, a dike of rocks and gravel faced with corrugated steel, maintains the level of Chamberlain Lake so that water flows south through Penobscot River hydroelectric dams. A large gate valve allows only barely-canoeable water to Eagle Lake. Standing beside the gate valve, I wondered how long it would be before safe nuclear-electric plants make hydroelectric plants obsolete. I hoped that Allagash water would again flow north as it did when it carried Indian canoes.

But the site was not all disappointment. While searching the bushes near the new dam, I found the remnants of the old one. The blacksmith-forged spike I turned up was much lighter than the paddle-boat steam engine down the lake. I now have a valued Allagash souvenir.

As I carried my rusty prize back across the dam I glanced at the dam keeper's camp. It looked familiar, but since I hadn't been there before, I thought my mind must be playing tricks on me. Suddenly I remembered. The camp, now with a new front porch, was featured on the dust cover of Dorothy Boone Kidney's *A Home in the Wilderness*. The book, which I recommend, describes Kidney's adventures when her husband was a keeper at Lock Dam. Isn't it great to recognize an old friend?

"Hey, Gramp," Alan called me back from another world, "let's set up camp." Good suggestion. The wind was increasing. Benign white clouds were developing tall cumulus towers and ragged gray bases.

Three generations soon had two tents pitched, a fire built in the rock campsite fireplace and a pot of dishwater on to boil. A kitchen fly tarp was stretched over a picnic table and supper was soon cooking on a gas stove. Fifteen-year-old Michael cooked, reminding me that kids grow up fast. With the water heated over the fireplace during the meal, washing and scalding the dishes was a short job.

Evening darkened quickly under the thickening clouds, and as lightning flashed across the lake I lay in a Nixon-Administration-vintage tent with two worries. The least was that the tent would leak. The second concern involved the approaching lightning bolts and the tall trees around the camp. I kept reminding myself that those bolts had thousands of trees to choose among and that it was a minor storm anyway. Because my worries did not materialize, I slept without complaining about the rocks and roots under my sleeping bag.

Next morning during breakfast, Dean Wiggins, the amiable Allagash Wilderness Waterway ranger now stationed at Lock Dam, stopped by for C and C (conversation and coffee). As Dean spun his yarns about places and things to see in the area, including an old Lombard log hauler in a brook where it had gotten mired 70 years ago, I realized that I needed five weeks instead of five days to "do" the Allagash. I couldn't do it all, but I did accompany Dean to his camp where I stood in the room in which Mrs. Kidney did some of her writing.

After breaking camp and loading our canoes below Lock Dam, we paddled the short, rocky narrow thoroughfare between Chamberlain and Eagle lakes. On those rocks are souvenirs of thousands of canoes—paint, exotic plastics and aluminum—red, green, blue, yellow. We added a touch of Old Town green.

The present elevation of Eagle Lake is close to the original. Indians saw it much as it is now. The Allagash Wilderness Waterway campsites may well have been places where Indians once camped. I am told that "Allagash" in their language meant "river of many hunting camps." If so, they chose their hunting grounds well.

I recognized the Bear Mountain area of Eagle Lake because I had been there in 1993 with the Maine Forest Service to put out a burning, lightning-struck tree. However, I didn't realize at the time that I was so close to Maine logging history. Michael, who had "done" the Allagash twice with Boy Scout friends, directed me into a cove from which large rocks had been moved to the shore, forming a log-holding area. Within a mile of the lightning strike, a short canal leads from the cove to tons of Maine logging history.

Because using dams and locks is a slow way to transfer logs from lake to lake, a steam-driven tramway was built in 1901. An endless 6,000-foot cable had two-wheel dollies bolted to it every 10 feet. Upper and lower rails were built through the 3,000 feet of woods between the lakes. On the Chamberlain Lake end, a steam engine drove the huge sprocket wheel that in turn drove the tramway cable. Logs were loaded onto the dollies at Eagle Lake, pulled over the upper rails and dumped into Chamberlain Lake. The dollies returned on the lower tracks. The tramway was used for six years before it was made obsolete by Lombard log haulers. Mature trees now grow among several tons of rusting steel.

Alvin Lombard's first log hauler was built at Waterville Ironworks in 1900 and patented in 1901. A steam engine (later, gasoline engines) drove two endless belts of steel lags long and wide enough for the machine to move on iced woods roads. Steered by front skis, the hauler was powerful enough to pull many loaded sleds over long distances to rivers and lakes. However, even though he used many log haulers, Edouard Lecroix's 1920s and 1930s crews cut so much wood in the area that he built a railroad 12 miles or so from the Eagle Lake tramway terminal to Umbazooksus Lake in Penobscot waters. Two railroad engines now rust in the woods at the Eagle Lake tramway terminal and mature trees grow among several dozen tons of rusting rails and rolling stock.

After a leisurely trip down Eagle Lake, through the thoroughfare to Churchill Lake, and down the lake past Churchill Ridge, we came to Jaws campsite at the lake outlet, where we went through our now familiar setup routine.

That evening I confessed to a fellow from New York who was sharing the campsite that even though I lived only 70 miles to the east, I had never canoed The River before. He understood, saying that he grew up in New York City but had never visited the Statue of Liberty until he moved away and returned for a visit.

Next morning our party motored a short distance down Heron Lake to Churchill Dam. There we placed our wangan on a pile behind that of other groups. Kim Lynch, an Allagash Waterway ranger, would portage our gear around Chase Rapids with a pickup.

Mark, the boys, and I walked over to what used to be Edouard Lecroix's Churchill Depot, the center of his logging operation, which once employed several thousand men. There used to be a huge garage, carpenter and blacksmith shops, a sawmill, storage buildings, houses for 20 or so families, a schoolhouse and the large boarding house.

Mark, who once worked in the area, pointed out a weedy field where he had helped load several Lombard log haulers onto flatbed trailers to be taken to museums. Just as at Chamberlain Farm, I felt that I had lost part of my heritage.

However, as at Chamberlain Farm, not all was lost. We met Tim Caverly, Allagash Wilderness Waterway supervisor, and his daughter Jacquelyn. Tim explained that most of the old buildings had been burned not only because they would have been too expensive to maintain, but also to improve the canoeists' wilderness experience. He said their home and the Waterway headquarters also had been built out of sight of the river to preserve the natural view. Tim's wife Sue is a clerk for the Waterway and her office is in their home.

With Tim tagging along, Jackie took us to see the old boarding house, which the Waterway folks hope to restore as a museum. When we saw it, the house had a rusting steel roof, nondescript weathered siding and boarded up windows. But new sills had been installed by those hoping to save a bit of our heritage.

Heritage, indeed. Jackie proudly showed us the inside. There is a drying room where thousands of longjohns, woolen hats, coats and pants, wool socks, mittens and boots have dried around a huge stove. There is a logging-camp-style cook room and dining room with crew tables and benches. Up narrow stairs from the cook room, the "ram pasture" occupies part of the upstairs. There are still smudges at cot height where greasy heads rubbed the walls at night. A regular pattern of nail holes marks where clothes hung. Such was a crew's sleeping quarters.

The other end of the top floor is divided into small rooms for guests and school teachers such as Helen Leidy, later Helen Hamlin. Once again, I stood in a room formally used by a favorite author. Years before, I had enjoyed Helen Hamlin's *Nine Mile Bridge* about her life in the area.

After persuading Jackie to write about the boarding house . . . and thanking her and Tim for the much appreciated tour, we returned to Churchill Dam and found that Kim had portaged our wangan, including the motor. The Waterway rangers have picked enough wangan out of Chase Rapids so they insist that they portage belongings for those who want to canoe the white water. Some elect to have the entire party portaged.

Speaking of retrieving wangan, a decision was made that will no doubt have reverberations for years. Michael and Alan persuaded their father that they had enough experience to canoe Chase Rapids below the dam, the swiftest white water on The River. Anxiously, Mark and I watched the boys paddle their canoe into the churning water. Shouting instructions to each other, they deftly avoided rocks and chose the best course as they sped along. We breathed with relief as they slipped the canoe around a river bend and into a quiet eddy.

It was our turn, and I sat in the bow of our canoe. Red hopped into center canoe and Mark sat in the stern (the navigator's seat), complaining as we pushed off, that the motor mount hindered his paddling. As we picked up speed in swift rough water, I heard Mark order a very nervous dog to "Sit!"

"Pull to the right of that rock!" He shouted to me. I paddled hard.

"No! No!" he yelled, "the other rock! Red—sit! Damn that motor mount!"

I pulled the other way—too late. We bumped the rock hard, tipping the canoe perhaps 30 degrees to the right, a problem that two experienced canoeists could have corrected. But a 200-plus-pound klutz in the front and a large jittery dog in the middle landed on the right gunwale. That was too much for the single good canoeist in the stern to handle, so we all came up wet.

We managed to manipulate the canoe to shallow water where we could dump it and reload. It took quite some time to get Red back in. Then we negotiated the rest of Chase Rapids to the boys' canoe without incident.

"Hey, what took you so long?" Alan wanted to know.

"Look," said Michael, they're wet! They dumped their canoe!"

They spent altogether too much time laughing at us. Michael offered to take the stern next time we ran Chase Rapids so the old people wouldn't get wet again. I will cherish that Allagash moment forever. I'm not sure about Mark, though.

An Allagash trip never runs out of memorable moments. A few miles downstream we stopped where Kim left our wangan to reload our canoes. A party from Rhode Island was excitedly taking pictures of a cow moose and her calf. When we continued our trip, we were swept past the two animals within a canoe's length. At Mark's command, Red minded his manners.

The high water made it possible for me to use our motor where we would normally have had to paddle. I tried to pay attention to my job, because The River from Chase Rapids to Umsaskis Lake was like a gigantic waterslide. However, bordered by green walls back-dropped by green ridges and canopied by blue sky, it is too big for an amusement park. Once we slowed to watch a bear, very black against the blue-grey water, fight the current as it crossed the river in front of us. Another time, a majestic brown bird, a gold eagle, I think, flew up the river over us at tree-top level not far upriver from Umsaskis Lake.

Running the motor on the slow water of Umsaskis Lake, barely ruffled by a slight breeze, demanded little attention. We watched ospreys fish. Waterfowl flew by. Loons, floating low in small waves, occasionally dived for fish, but seemed unconcerned about us. The bright reds, blues and yellows of beached canoes and pitched tents at campsites stood out against the solid walls of green along the shores.

It was with great satisfaction that I approached the steel Reality Road bridge (at mile 56 on the 92-mile Reality Road from Ashland, Maine, to Daaquam, Québec) at the Umsaskis-to-Long Lake thoroughfare. Often when I crossed the bridge while traveling for the Maine Forest Service I had watched canoeists pass under it and longed to "do The River" sometime. That day was that sometime—and I had the next two generations with me.

Long Lake is well-named. Perhaps we most enjoyed the motor as opposed to a long, long paddle here, because we could lie back and relax into our own worlds. Probably the boys and Mark recall Long

Lake incidents from other trips. I remembered seeing arrowheads and Indian scraping tools collected from the area. Since the Long Lake log-driving dam washed out years ago, the water level has returned essentially to that the Indians knew. I thought I would not want to move Indian artifacts; they belong where their makers lived.

The white man's artifacts are also still there. Rotting boom logs and rusting logging equipment aren't hard to find. Brooks, lakes and campsites are named for those who worked there: Sweeney, Cunliffe, Grey, Harding, Jalbert, Shepherd, Glazier. When we passed Chemquasabamticook Stream, I recalled that the McNally Camps, a few dozen yards upstream were soon to pass their 100th year in the same family.

My mind went back on the job when we stopped to look at the pitch of water at Long Lake Dam. It was somewhat dangerous there because a few steel spikes are sticking out of the old dam base logs. We had enough water, so we did not have to portage.

After slipping over the dam carrying the motor in a canoe, we again found that we had a motorable pitch. The 10 miles or so of the river from Long Lake to Round Pond are not as fast as the Churchill-to-Umsaskis water. In places I had to switch my attention from animals, birds and scenery to sandbars; low, bushy islands; rocks; and an occasional dead tree stuck in the river.

If that stretch of The River is a challenge, Round Pond certainly compensates for it. Resting at The Inlet campsite, I marveled at the many shades of green woods that rose from the lake shore over layer after layer of ridges and small mountains to a clear blue sky. Blue and white kingfishers and red-winged blackbird's provided contrasting flashes of color against the greens. And all this was doubled by reflections from calm spots on the pond. Gentle breezes ripped first this spot then that, giving the illusion of a gigantic paintbrush leaving streak after streak of silver on the pond.

"Hey, Gramp," Alan called, "let's set up camp so I can go fishing." He has his priorities right. I helped him while supper was cooked and wood split.

After the dishes were done, the same scene that had captivated me was tinted by an orange sunset. With no air movement, Round Pond became a mirror. A strange illusion made a low-flying duck appear to be under water. A dragonfly hovering just over the surface seemed to be looking at itself in the mirror. A loon paddled slowly by; its wake, two widening wave lines, ended in an expanding ring when the bird went under water. Then the wake settled back into the orange mirror.

The campfire glowed brighter as darkness approached. The boys fished. Mark and I enjoyed an extra cup of coffee. Red looked for one last squirrel to chase. The Allagash was the way it was supposed to be, especially Round Pond.

In the morning, with canoes separated, we passed through Round Pond rips. It is a strange, exhilarating sensation to ride a canoe down a fairly steep grade. I imagined Indian youngsters laboriously paddling birch bark canoes upstream just to ride the river back down. Why not? Kids pull sleds up long hills just to ride them back down, don't they?

With canoes reattached, our little motor made the trip down miles of dead water leisurely and relaxing. Moose and an occasional deer seldom retreated into the surrounding woods as we passed. Clouds gathered, giving the impression we were traveling in an enclosed green canyon. We sometimes surprised ducks, geese and seagulls when we slid past low, grassy, bush islands.

A well-tanned young ranger motored on the river from his camp at Michaud Farm. We cut our motor and floated as he checked our Waterway permit and made sure we understood we must portage around Allagash Falls. Good advice indeed!

We continued down river, weaving with the channel around large, tree-covered islands. The clouds began to look ugly and rising winds fishtailed back and forth across the river. There was sharp lightning with accompanying thunder to our north. We decided to hurry to an Allagash Falls campsite rather than wait out the storm on an island. But the edge of the storm caught us, so we were wet when we landed, unloaded our canoes and stretched a protecting kitchen fly tarp over a picnic table. Peanut butter sandwiches, even without coffee, never tasted better. The roar of the falls and punctuating thunder were not figures of speech.

The rain more or less stopped and the portage began. Alan and I carried waterproof boxes and bags of wangan over the few hundred yards of portage trail. Michael and Mark carried heavier equipment and canoes.

As tired, wet and sore as I was, I could not escape a collective presence on that portage. There were Indian artifacts just under the soil, I was certain. Tribes could not have used that trail for all those years without losing pottery, arrows, obsidian knives, stones gouges and perhaps, in later years, metal tools. There were protruding edges of steel logging something-or-others left more recently. There were deep scrapes in the rocks parallel with the trail made by loggers hauling heavy loads of equipment. There was a heavy steel ring wedged and leaded into ledge, strategically located for ropes and pulleys to drag those heavy loads up the steepest incline. From more recent years, there were scraps of nylon rope and exotic, colored cloth and the familiar red, green, yellow, blue and aluminum canoe scrapings.

A lightning bolt and immediate jarring thunder switched my attention from the trail up through the trees to the cloud above. I have seen B-52 bombers fly with their bomb bay doors open over the electronic strategic training range west of Ashland. Looking up into that cloud gave me the same ominous impression of potential danger as did looking up into those open bomb bays.

Alan and I ran for the kitchen fly, but the downpour caught us. We were wet again, but we figured we were better off sitting under the tarp on a larger picnic table then cramped under a canoe on the other end of the portage as we guessed Michael and Mark were. Later they said they had indeed been cramped under a canoe—and happy that it did not leak.

The cloud and violent weather front passed quickly. As we reloaded our canoes below the falls, a painful loss was discovered. A forester, Mark had worked and camped with a favorite ax for years. The ax was back at Round Pond, and no amount of fuming could change that.

The long day, a number of portage trips around Allagash Falls, and getting wet several times wore on me. In the quick water below the falls, my arms and shoulders didn't move my paddle well. Fortunately, 15-year-old Michael, seated in the stern, negotiated frothy waves, rocks and cross currents easily. Even so, I was glad to use the stretch of quiet water to reattach the outboard motor.

With weather clearing behind the violent front, a warm dry jacket over a wet shirt and an industrious propeller doing the work, the trip downriver to Big Brook East campsite was pleasant. A short distance below where we intended to land, a magnificent bull moose stood shoulder deep, feeding in the river. I stopped the motor early and we watched him as the two canoes drifted quietly toward the shore. His head was thrust underwater after aquatic plants. When the muscular body lifted his head, water streamed from his broad antlers. He paid us little heed. We were only guests in his Allagash home.

I was grateful to be sharing that home for a few days. But being grateful notwithstanding, carrying our wangan up the steep river bank to the campsite was difficult. The tents were pitched a little more slowly than usual. As the boys and Mark set up the kitchen fly and utensils, I split wood. The inside of solid wood was the only thing in that universe that was even somewhat dry. Using the best grade of Boy Scout woodsmanship, Mark coaxed a match flame into a most welcome campfire.

As Alan and I sat by the fire turning now and then so the heat would dry us all around, I was amazed at the stamina of Mark and Michael. After the day we had, they cooked supper and joked as casually as they had cooked breakfast and joked. After the meal we sat and talked as gathering darkness shrunk our world to the tents, kitchen fly and tree branches around our campfire.

When I suggested it was past my bedtime, Michael said: "Hey, wait, Gramp, this is our last night on the river. I'm going to cook doughnuts for a treat." Tired or not, I was not about to pass that up. The doughnuts and another pot of coffee were easily worth the wait. But Michael had no takers for several deep-fat-fried mosquitoes.

In the morning, the skies were blue again for our last day on the river. As we motored the last few miles toward Allagash village, sometimes, as at Twin Brook Rapids, the channel narrowed and gray-white frothy waves rushed up past green-conifer walls. At other times, the river slowed and braided itself among low islands anchored by splendid hardwoods. Those islands needed their anchors. Ice-out gouges in tree bark were often six feet or more above summer water levels.

Soon signs of permanent habitation became common. Upstream from Allagash village, a road that parallels the river seemed in places to be so low that the spring ice-out must flow over it. Several houses along the river were built on safe, high ground. Television antennas seemed totally out of place. A blackened forest-fire scar reminded us that we are lucky to have our upper Allagash River basin in such fine condition.

At the village we unloaded our wangan for the last time (only for that trip, I hope) and placed it beside the highway along with our canoes. Only then did we realize that we'd missed a golf-ball-sized hail storm (rare in northern Maine) the day before. Windows were broken, roofs destroyed, vehicles pockmarked and gardens flattened.

"Hey, Gramp," Allen said, "we'd have had to get under that picnic table at Allagash Falls if the hail hit there."

I agreed that the kitchen fly probably wouldn't have protected us.

"Hey, Gramp," he added, grinning, "we'd have been sitting in about six inches of muddy ice water for an hour or so. I guess this trip wasn't all that bad."

That trip wasn't all that bad. Indeed.

Postscript: My friends at Allagash Maine Forest Service Headquarters radioed the Allagash Wilderness Waterway folks that a cherished ax had been left at Round Pond. It was turned in at Michaud Farm within a day or so. Mark was notified by telephone and retrieved his prized possession. That's the way things are on the Allagash.

Way Back *When...*

Musings

by Marjorie Bishop

Dad's Surprises

We were always glad when our Dad's job "tied up" in Presque Isle. In railroad terms it means "stopped work at the end of a day." That meant he would probably be home for supper. On these days he walked home after work and he always stopped at Buswell's General Store in the Porter Block, at the corner of State and Mechanic Streets. He called home from the store to see if Mom needed anything.

Suppers on those days were always with the entire family around the dining room table. After the meal was over, one of us would find Dad's jacket, retrieve a bulging paper bag and bring it to the table. Then we enjoyed its contents—usually "penny candy" from Albert's Store.

We all enjoyed the treat of penny candy. One of our favorites was a "Bo-Hunk." I don't know if that was its real name or just one we made up. It was an inch square of peanuts and caramel dipped in chocolate. I have searched for them to no avail. The closest I have found is the Snickers bar. No wonder we liked it so much!

Safe!

One day my dad was riding from Presque Isle to Mapleton. He was in the caboose and as they left Presque Isle they traveled through the wet swampy land near outer Mechanic Street. As he glanced out the window, he saw three small children in the water. It was a dangerous place for them to play. He telegraphed back to the station agent, told him to send the section crew to get them. They did. After they had been checked out and reunited with their parents, there were two very grateful families in town that day.

They expressed their gratitude to my dad many, many times thereafter.

R.W. Wight

My father once worked in the R.W. Wight Furniture Store. He was young and could handle the lifting, pushing, and pulling that their stock required. In one instance he fell down the service elevator shaft. He got up and walked away with only a few bruises.

Milk Toast

In my parents' home milk toast came to the table on a platter piled high with the slices, buttered, and covered with white sauce between the slices and dripping down the sides.

Where I boarded in Caribou it was different, but just as delicious, and the way I still make it. It's quick and easy—two buttered slices covered with about ¼ cup of warmed cream (I use half 'n half). Try it, you'll like it.

First Trip to Boston

My first trip to Boston was with other family members to pick up my grandparents who were returning from a few weeks in Florida.

I remember a side trip to Newport, Rhode Island. The husband of our host family worked there. We saw all the sights and walked on the boardwalk that had been constructed between the sandy beach and the row of very large houses. They were mansions to me.

Citizenship

My mother was born in the U. S. of A. When she married my father she became a Canadian by law. She remained so for many years. My father became a naturalized citizen in due course. One would think this would return his wife to her original status. Not so! She still was an "alien" and had to register as such for many more years. After much correspondence and red tape she was never repatriated.

Traveling to Teach

The Aroostook Valley Railroad once had an electric car that went from Presque Isle to Caribou via Crouseville and Washburn. It went by the end of our street and the conductor was a neighbor. On Monday mornings I walked to the track. He stopped the trolley and I got a ride to my teaching position. When we arrived I walked up the hill to the private home where I had a room. My landlords were an elderly couple. I had breakfast with them each day, lunch in the Caribou High School cafeteria, and the night meal at the "Stop 'n' Shop," a small restaurant. When Friday evening came, I walked down the hill in the opposite direction to the Bangor and Aroostook Station and returned back home for the weekend.

The previously mentioned elderly couple was of the Christian Science faith and their church services were held in their living room.

Paternal Grandmother

My paternal grandmother was a remarkable person. She had little formal schooling but was self-taught. She learned along with her children when they brought home their homework. She saw that each played at least one instrument and each had an education beyond high school. Her brood had teachers, a hairdresser, a banker, a railroad conductor/brakeman, a nurse, and a mortician. And they could all sing. When the Canadian relatives visited they always had hymn sings. Gram was a very religious person. She insisted on church attendance.

One of my gram's sisters went to live with the Indians. She learned all about healing with nature's medicinal products and became a "virtual medicine woman."

Skating on Presque Isle Stream

I spent many hours each winter at the skating rink. I loved the sport and was quite good at it. Beside the Presque Isle stream above the State Street Bridge, the town maintained the rink and a warming hut. My grandfather, in his later years, lived in a rooming house beside the stream, from Downing's Lumber Mill. Often this gave me a convenient place to get warm and to get into and out of my skating gear.

Dad Outdoors

My Dad loved the outdoors. He did all those things our county is noted for—fishing, hunting, gardening and the like. In the winter he always built us a slide in the back corner of our lot. He hauled snow from the front yard to the back and finally had a large snow hill. He built a sluiceway from it through our backyard and the neighbor's side yard to the street. He also kept up a slide on the front lawn, which had a gradual slope, for the younger kids. This made a great playground for all ages. Youngsters in our area came to our yard to play.

My Brothers

I had three younger brothers. We grew up loving each other and being proud of one another. The oldest brother was a marine and an atomic warrior. He survived the war, came home, and worked at Northern National Bank. He later joined his wife's family's business. The second brother survived the Korean War. He also joined the Northern National Bank. Later he joined the Federal Reserve Bank of Boston as a bank examiner. My youngest brother joined the Navy. He and his family lived in Pensacola, Spain and Guam. He finally finished his career in Washington at the Pentagon.

The Spoon

My brothers and I all had our own silverware sets—knife, fork, and spoon. They were smaller than regular and each was a different pattern. Through the years they all disappeared except for one brother's spoon. It ended up at my house among my eating utensils.

We buried my brother last week so I gave the spoon to his widow. He requested that some of his ashes be put in the Allagash and on our parents' grave. While fulfilling this last request his wife and daughter had a plant to leave on the grave, but they had no digging tool. Fortuitously I had supplied them with just what they needed.

Games

On summer nights after supper the kids would gather at the large telephone pole halfway down the street. It was our GOAL for running games such as Hide and Seek. "It" would count while the rest of us hid. We tried to get back to the goal without being tagged by "It." At dusk our parents would tell us that it was time to come on in by switching on the porch light. We in turn would signal our playmates by calling "All-y, all-y in Free."

Grandson Bill Graduates

Graduation was approaching. Getting a Guest Speaker was up to my grandson, Bill Fletcher, the senior class president at Calais High School. Since the Governor, Angus King and his wife Mary Hermon with children Ben and Molly, were longtime friends, why not ask him? It was arranged that The First Lady would do the honors as he was unavailable. He made it however and delivered a short speech also. Afterward we all gathered back at home and enjoyed the rest of the day visiting with each other. We grandparents went off to the motel leaving our room and bed so that the executive family could sleep under the one roof.

Grandfather's Land

My grandfather once owned the land on the right side of State Street, beyond the Park Gate. He sold frontage for businesses and homes and farmed the rest. The farmhouse for this land was farther down on State Street. The family moved from Maysville to this location. Changes were made prior to the move or afterward, I'm not sure. Anyway, he made the barn the house and the house the barn. When the family moved again he did the same thing. He remodeled the barn and made a bigger and better house. The house, now the barn, was later moved to an adjacent lot for the eldest daughter and her husband.

Gramp, a Mover and Shaker

When the airport became important to the air force and they needed extra land, they took the rest of the farm from behind Turner

Street to the brook. That meant moving more houses. Gramp did it. There are at least five houses now on Turner Street and one on Wilson Avenue that were once beyond the park gate. It intersected the road built parallel to the brook back to State Road.

The house that went to Wilson Avenue was the first one we lived in before Dad built our permanent home on Turner Street.

In jest I called my gramp a "mover and a shaker" partly because of the preceding anecdote and partly because he was a deputy sheriff. I can picture some people trembling as he approached them.

Park Street House

The house on Park Street was the only one I remember. The inside had a few unusual features. All four bedrooms on the second floor had walk-in closets. They were large and had slanting ceilings. The women loved them.

The stairway came down in the middle, but not all the way to the first floor. A landing was built up from the first floor to meet the stairs. That left openings on both the living room and the bedroom side. Stairs were built up to the landing from each room. There were about four for each room for easy access. On the bedroom side some of the stairs were hinged and opened up a cubby hole for storage. I remember one thing in there—a pair of ladies high-buttoned shoes with a button hook.

At the partition between the living room and the dining room there were two short walls jutting out into the space between them. This divided them and left a large open space between them. At the room end of each short wall was a baluster rising from wall to ceiling. These were like fancy newel posts but many times larger.

On the side porch was a gathering place with a large hammock and assorted chairs. It was a great place to swing or sleep during the day and evenings after the supper meal. It was where problems were solved and accomplishments were acknowledged.

There is one more thing about this house that was once a barn. The cellar stairs went down from the kitchen. At the end, and to the left, was a large wooden cover with a bailing rope covering the top of a large well.

Turning a Phrase

My husband Dana H. Bishop could, as they say, "turn a phrase." By what he said or did often changed gloom-and-doom sadness to happiness; bad to good, etc. Our sixty-three years together were full of fun and laughter. For example, when the cardiac nurse was discussing diet with him, he said, "Oh, no pie! My wife makes the best pie crust east of the Mississippi." And when a neighbor said he and his wife would drop by to see us he said, "You better call first so we will be sure to have our clothes on."

And there was the time I took him to the E.R. and they decided to keep him. He asked them to get me home. It was after midnight. So the nurse called Leisure Village. The doctor went to the E.R. and got the officer there to take me to our door. Meantime, one of the aides at the Village was dispatched to the E.R. to get me. He couldn't find me anywhere. At last he went to my husband's hospital room to see if I was there. "No," my husband said. "The cops came and took her away." Most of the time his "way with words" delighted our family and friends. (Not that this was our lifestyle, but he said it anyway.)

Mother's Horse

My mother grew up in very comfortable circumstances. She enjoyed many things the rest of us just wished for. One was her own riding horse. She rode him everywhere. He was a very obedient pet and most always obeyed her.

At what is now the intersection of State, Parsons, Dyer, and Mechanic Streets in Presque Isle, there was a large circular watering trough for large animals. Coming or going, Mom's pet horse never passed it without stopping for sustenance, whether his rider wanted to stop or not.

Eye Problems

Along with the usual eye problems of aging, I have Charles Bonet Syndrome. It is not a bad thing. It's an illusion when an image appears in your vision. My "visitors" are two playing cards—The King and the Jack of a red suit. They come and go so quickly that I can't tell whether they are hearts or diamonds!

Algonquin Hotel

As president of the Maine State Bar association our son-in-law hosted members at the Algonquin Hotel in St. Andrews, New Brunswick. It was their annual meeting and well attended. Although not members, we went along to babysit our two grandchildren while their parents tended to their obligations. We explored the resort with them and had an enjoyable time in the "Duke of Wales Royal Suite" where the family was housed for the weekend.

Northern Maine Fair

The Northern Maine Fair was a great occasion. I started young. My father would carry me to see the animal exhibits. As I grew older, I would submit items of embroidery or samples of cooking to see if I could win a prize. When I grew older still, my uncle would hire me to help in his food booth. One year, in my first trip around the exhibition halls, I came to the town photographer's display. I looked up and there staring down at me was a nearly life-sized enlargement of my graduation picture. (The photographer was "Brown.")

Remedies

Our good health was a prime concern of our parents. We had regular appointments with our doctor and dentist. We had home remedies in between.

In our cellar-way Dad built a hanging shelf for the breadbox and cookie tins. Dad also found room there for bottles of cod liver oil, Scott's Emulsion and others. Dad would sit four of us on the cellar steps to await our daily doses. So, to say we disliked sitting on the cellar stairs was putting it mildly.

Nature's Bounty

Nature's bounty was good to us each spring. First were the dandelions, which we seldom ate. Then the fiddleheads picked at our uncle's farm on the Washburn Road. These we relished and we ate them in abundance. A little later in early summer, we picked many wild raspberries on another uncle's farm on the back Caribou Road. I mustn't forget maple sugaring time. Our grandfather always set up a sugaring camp and tapped the trees. He boiled sap down in big kettles. He often took some partially boiled sap home and my grandmother finished it off on the kitchen stove and bottled it.

The Old Ring

The first three grandchildren were boys. The fourth was a girl who lived downstate. I came next and I stayed in the area—all my life, as a matter of fact. As the only girl close by, I got lots of attention from my grandparents and doting aunts and uncles. I was the recipient of their largess. This included time and travel with them, piano and voice lessons, wonderful family get-to-gathers. One gift I remember. It was an old ring that my aunt gave me, that her aunt had previously given her. As I entered my teens I noticed someone else wearing my ring. I spoke of it to my donor. It was retrieved. When I went through high school I wore the old ring with its five diamond chips daily.

Piano Lessons

When I started piano lessons we had no piano. After school each day, I would go to my grandparents' to practice. It was just across the street from my school. After a few years of this, a business associate bought a new piano for his girls. My gramp bought their old one for me.

Traveling to Belfast

My Dad was first a farmer, then a teacher, and then a railroad brakeman/conductor. He was with the Bangor and Aroostook (B&A)

from 1918 to 1962, retired in 1962, and died at the age of 99. Because of his affiliation with the railroad, my mother had a lifetime pass.

When she traveled I often went along. Soon my parents thought I was old enough to travel alone on a pass.

During school vacations I did just that. Most trips were to Belfast, where I spent most summers with a favorite uncle and aunt. I took the Bangor and Aroostook to Bangor. They would meet me or I would take McLaughlin's Bus Line and get to their home in Belfast on my own. I boarded the bus at the Exchange Hotel for the rest of the trip. Their route was Bangor to Rockland. I was sometimes the only passenger.

Moncton

One of my childhood friends had grandparents who lived near Moncton, New Brunswick. They occasionally took me along. They lived on a saltwater farm. In Salisbury, N.B., a natural phenomenon occurs there at high tide called Bore Tide or Tidal Bore. When the tide reaches the narrow river mouth, it builds up and forces copious amounts of water into the small opening. It's like a great waterfall racing upstream. There is a deafening roar that accompanies it. This wall of water continues upstream until it finally fits in between the banks.

Mother's Birth

The year was 1897. The season was Christmas. The place was Nashville Plantation. Dan and Minnie with their young daughters were spending a few days with her MacCormack relatives at their farm, which was the first farm on the left after leaving Ashland going toward Portage Lake. Many of you will know it as the residence of Sarah Brooks.

On December 30, 1897 my mother decided to be born. She was a few months premature and she weighed in at one-and-a-half pounds. She was kept warm in the large oven at the top of the kitchen cook stove in the second floor front corner bedroom on the side of the house facing Portage. Mother and daughter continued to do well. My mother grew up in a happy family on State Street in Presque Isle until she was thirteen, when her mother died.

After marrying my father, she lived a quiet, social life, enjoying bridge club, raised four children, and lived to the great age of eighty-nine.

Sewage Failure

Not all the things that happened were good. One such instance was when the sewage system at a neighbor's house failed. My maternal grandmother and her eldest daughter went next door to help clean up. The sad result was that both came down with Typhoid Fever. My dad was a teenager at the time and he told of the pitiful cries that came from the suffering going on next door. My aunt survived, but my grandmother did not.

Ice Cream

We had the hens and the eggs, Gramp had the cow and the cream—the basics for homemade ice cream. My mother made the custard. My father assembled the equipment. My brothers and I supplied the manpower for the wooden, hand-cranked machine. In summer we worked on the back steps with a block of ice from the iceman. In winter we used the snow from our large yard. It took about an hour of churning and a little help from the adults. Dad then took off the paddle and packed it again in the covered freezer with heavy insulation to preserve the contents. The last thing was to check our results by cleaning off the paddle. Yum! Yum!

Root Beer

At least once during the summer our parents would make us a special treat. It was home-made root beer. They would mix it, bottle and cap it, then stand the bottles on the floor next to the stove and under the hot water tank beside it. They let it sit there for the required time, then transferred it to shelves in our cellar where it stayed cool until an extra hot day came along or some special event occurred.

Locked In

Help! I can't get out. My bedroom door was shut and I was locked inside! Nothing I did on the inside or that my mother did on the outside worked. My dad was at work. My uncle and aunt lived down the street. My uncle came and took the door off its hinges, then broke the lock. I was "Free at last!"

Travel

After the service the oldest two brothers stayed on the farm to help get their parents' business reinvigorated. It took about a year. We moved to town and settled down to new lives. We traveled during school vacations with our small trailer. There were trips to Fundy Park, Prince Edward Island, Montreal and Quebec, and various places in Maine. These sojourns included our daughter and her lifelong friend, the one who, as she "left home" in her downstairs apartment, always came upstairs to our apartment.

One of our favorite camping spots was at the East Branch of the Penobscot. We would park our trailer there and then take side trips. One of them was to South Branch Pond. In those days this was easily one of the most beautiful spots in the state. We arrived there one day and found a snake curled up on the dock. As the girls wanted to play there, we threw a few rocks toward it to scare it away. Alas one rock hit it. Play area was secure.

Back at camp another day we were at the riverbed where the girls were hopscotching on the flat rocks. Suddenly word came that they were opening the dam. Soon the water would reach us. The rush was on to scurry up the bank to safety.

Fortuneteller

At least once every summer my mother and her friends would take a trip to Plaster Rock, New Brunswick to see a fortuneteller. Occasionally they would take their pre-teen daughters along. I don't think we believed what the seeress told us but we had fun. We enjoyed the companionship, the ride, and especially lunch at York's Tea Room in Andover.

Winter Vacation

One year during our winter vacation, I was invited with three other girl classmates to our teacher's farm home. It was near enough so we could walk there. We carried our lunch and continued through their yard to the woods on the back of their farm. We spent the day there in their rustic camp. After a day of fun and games, we walked back to the farmhouse where a delicious meal awaited us. To climax a perfect day, her brother harnessed one of the horses to the pung. Soon we were driven home in style. These same four girls were lucky enough to be invited back for several winters thereafter.

From a Christmas Card

Talk about being oblivious!!! Last week my daughter told me she had bought a rustic frame and was going to re-frame a piece of artwork. It seems that years ago my mother had asked her to sketch a homey scene on a piece of fabric. My mother would then embroider it. I don't remember anything about its production or its hanging in either of their homes. Where was I???

Greater than Grandchildren

If there's anything greater than grandchildren, it's great-grandchildren. I have seven. They are the very best in the world, but I try not to say so to others who also have some. If we cede first place to the one we're with, we can take it back later. "To each his own!"

Debating Team

In my junior year in high school, I was one of the debating team representing Presque Isle High School. I needed a new dress. My mother and I went to Pipes Clothing Store. It became a choice between a black skirt with a black velvet tunic and a wine colored coatdress. The black won out. But—my mother bought some wine velveteen and made me a near replica of the one I left behind. Incidentally, the subject for debate back then was "bicameral versus unicameral government." They are still debating it in Washington.

Grandfather's Boston

My grandfather was one of the suppliers of a large fur store in Boston, Kakas Co. He went back and forth to market as the season demanded. While in Boston he visited with his brother who was chief bookbinder at the Boston Public Library. A family story has it that Gramp did an advertisement or an endorsement for Doan's Pills on one of his trips to Boston.

Business Connections

My Grandfather was not only a fur dealer; he also dealt in other livestock. Our cellar was often full of pelts and furs of all kinds awaiting shipment. One time I remember he had a small flock of sheep penned in our garage. Among them was one black woolly lamb that I wanted to keep as a pet. My parents said, "No," I imagine it was said in much the same way as we would say today, "No way!"

Another business connection my grandfather had was with a Mr. Atkins, the well-known trapper and woodsman. Their arrangement was friendship with mutual respect and trust. After a winter in the woods, Trapper Atkins would bring his winter's work out to Oxbow. He would call my grandfather who would head to Oxbow on the Bangor and Aroostook Railroad. There the exchange of money and furs was finalized.

I didn't know about this until a friend brought it to my attention in an article by Mr. Leonard Hutchins in *Trapper's Magazine*, now a neighbor in Leisure Village and part of our writing group.

Mother and Dad Retire

My mother was in the nursing home when Dad was hospitalized for various reasons. When he was released, he too moved into the nursing home instead of going home. At that time Albert Cyr was giving much thought to building Leisure Gardens. Soon plans for the Gardens were real.

Albert thought it was not right that people should pay for nursing care they did not need. My dad was such a person. So Albert took the plans for Leisure Gardens to my dad and told him to pick out the apartment he wanted. He did just that. It was the one on the left as you enter the north entrance. He lived there eleven years until he was 99 years old.

Sports Fans

My family members are sports fans. It started with our school teams, then the town teams, and now the TV teams—Red Sox and Patriots. The three of us would attend most home games. Our daughter would find her chums and go right to the cheering section. We would go left to mid-court and climb up to the top row of the bleachers. Baseball games were played in the part in the field encircled by the racetrack. At fair time we attended the races. We sat in a box seat in the front of the grandstand with a fair director and his family.

Flight

In 1945 I took my one and only airplane ride. The flight was from Presque Isle to Boston with several stops in between. I got off in Houlton for a day of shopping. I returned home by bus the same afternoon. If you think this is a bit strange, as I do, consider this—I have never ridden a bicycle.

Miramichi

My husband took me on one of his Miramichi fishing trips. It was my first time in the area. Our guide was excellent and took care that our needs were met. Except for one thing, the buzzing, biting, flying bugs and insects which swarmed about us. We used all the traditional deterrents such as nets and fly dope. I even tried smoking for the first and only time in my life. As a result I never went back to these fishing spots and never smoked again.

Moxie Man

The soft drink Moxie has been around awhile. A man in Union, Maine created it in the 1870's.

Early on the company did some advertising. One was a favorite of mine: It was the Horse-Mobile that consisted of a model horse mounted on a platform. The Moxie Man sat astride the horse and drove the "float" along parade routes. In those days we had an occasional circus and always on the opening day of the annual fair, a parade was part of the program.

We lived near the State Street entrance of the fairgrounds. It was an ideal spot to view the parade either coming or going. We had been told that the Moxie Man once lived in the Presque Isle area. That made him all the more interesting. The Moxie Horse is now owned by a Japanese Company.

July 11, 2016

Last Saturday night, July 9, I was listening to the news on Channel 2 when I heard the word "Moxie." They were telling about a special celebration of "Moxie Days" somewhere in central Maine. They would be featuring the soft drink and its discoverer.

That same night, and in the very next program, "Bill Green's Maine," he was doing a special about the Miramichi! I was intrigued, because within the previous three months, I had written these two stories for the Writer's Group. Coincidental—perhaps. Fortuitous—maybe. Unusual—for sure.

Extended Families

My two extended families lived side by side on State Street in Presque Isle. Their lives were very similar in lots of ways. Both were large families. My Gram married "H.B.," that's what she called him, in Jacksontown, N.B. He had two girls from a previous marriage. My dad was my Gram's first child. They moved to Maine when he was quite young. There followed a family of four more girls and one boy.

My mother's family consisted of four girls and three boys. There was fun and harmony as these children grew up.

Then tragedy. My mom's mother died. Later my gramp brought a new wife to the scene. The original family was very upset. Some of them left home. Those remaining resented this person and there was bitterness on both sides, so much so that another girl left to live with a neighbor.

The new wife died when her first child—a boy—was born. My grandfather took the baby to a young couple and boarded him there. He stayed with this family until he himself got married. The family had contact with him through the years. He was absorbed into the "fold." He and his siblings agreed to let bygones be bygones.

Aunt Flo

Aunt Flo was probably the best piano accompanist of the family. My gramp always went to get her when the Canadian relatives came for a hymn-sing. She lived outside of town near Hobart Hill with her husband who was recovering from tuberculosis. She also helped with the care, in later years, when my gramp was bedridden. She was quite a wit and tried to lighten up the sick room. One day she said to him, "Shitie on the shirt tail, ten cents extra." When he roused a bit, she had the response she was after.

Locked Out

Earlier I wrote about being locked in. Today I'm writing about being locked out. This happened here at Leisure Village after my husband died. Every caregiver who came along tried to fit a key into the lock. Nothing worked. Soon the manager came, but his key was useless too. He left for a few minutes. Soon my door opened and he was in my kitchen holding the door open for us.

He had gone outside, taken the screen off one of my living room windows, opened the window and climbed in.

The screen was never put back. I'm all for leaving it that way—just in case.

Bank Stock

After our parents had all of us educated and we were out on our own, they found they occasionally had a few extra dollars. My father invested them in bank stock. Each time this happened, he put half of the shares in my mother's name and half in his. My mom was a stay-at-home mom and never worked outside the home. Thus she never had a pay check. This arrangement proved what we already knew—he was wise, thoughtful and caring. His plan gave her an income from the dividend checks, which she used any way she wanted. This continued until she was unable to handle her own affairs.

PERSISTENCE
by Maxine Smith

My mother's life was a classic example of persistence. Her childhood must have had some influences that helped her to develop this trait early in life, as her youth, her young adulthood, and her senior years all showed a strong persistent nature. Throughout her life, an outstanding quality of her character was the persistence that she manifested.

As a young girl, she was determined to get an education. In the small town of Masardis where she lived, there was a two-year high school, which my mother entered at age twelve. She worked hard and finished the two years and began to investigate ways to continue. The town would pay tuition wherever a student attended, so the problem was to find a place to live in the town where a four-year high school existed. When school opened that fall, she sadly realized she was not going to be able to continue school, so she looked for and found a job as house-helper in a neighboring settlement. During the winter she came to spend a weekend at home and found an aunt and uncle visiting. They lived in Mapleton, a town with a new four-year high school. When they learned that this young girl, only fourteen, was not in school they asked "Why?" The answer was a wistful, "I have no place to live." An invitation to come and work her board in their home was forthcoming. She *would* be back to continue her education the following year. She had persisted and won the opportunity to continue high school and graduate.

After graduation from high school, this young woman was offered an opportunity to teach at a rural school, which was allowed then, if the teacher would take a six-week course at the local Normal School. My mother wanted to do just that, but could not raise the money for the tuition. She had fallen in love and was being pressured by the young man to get married. Teachers were scarce, and soon the superintendent came to tell her that she *could* teach without the six weeks training. Mother and Dad married in August of 1920, and Mom thought she would be teaching that fall. However, Dad decided that no self-respecting husband would allow his wife to work outside the home. Mom's dream of being a teacher went on "hold" for nearly thirty years while she raised a family of four, three of whom became teachers!

At age 53, Mom was widowed. A son who was working on his master's at Orono convinced her that she should go to summer school with him and if she decided, to begin work that fall on a degree in teaching. She did just that and by attending the year around, she graduated in three years with a degree in English. In the fall of 1957 she began her teaching career at Ashland High School as an English teacher. She was 56 years old! Persistence had won her a realization of her dream.

Because Mom was interested in teaching long enough to earn a decent pension, and because she loved her work, she taught until she was seventy years old. That must have been one time when she said, "I will persist."

When she finally retired, she decided to travel. She drove her car about everywhere in this country and even flew to Europe for three weeks to visit eight countries there. Then she spent her winters in Florida and summers in Ashland until her death at 80 years. I think she persisted until the end, because a diagnosis of cancer and three months to live did not daunt her. She decided to spend the time in Florida and made it last *eleven* months. On one of her final days she saw my tears and said, "Look, daughter, don't cry for me. I have had a wonderful life. I have done all the things I wanted to do. I have so many good memories."

On The Wire Line
by William McConnell

In the 1920's, the forest fire detection towers at Hedgehog, Carr Pond, and Debouli Mountains were connected with each other and the nearest towns with a telephone line strung through insulators and hung on trees along existing roads used by lumbermen. A telephone hooked up to this line was powered by dry cells in the phone. The system might be compared to electric fencing in that the line must be kept isolated from anything that would shunt the phone energy to ground.

Seasonal tree growth and the occasional tree fallen across the line, required linemen to walk the line each year to clear away anything touching it. Midway on a line running from a cabin at Fish River Falls to Debouli Mountain tower, along the Chapman Toteroad, a small log cabin had been built to allow an overnight stay.

Linemen Joe Tardie and Ora Daggett have arrived at the cabin. Ora has gone back to the falls cabin for some reason but is expected back. Joe has gone to bed on the top bunk at dusk. Aroused by the sound of rattling tin dishes, he speaks: "*Attend Hora, I make a light.*" He scratches a match, to see that his visitor is not Ora but a bear, that, at the sound of his voice and the flash of light, beats a hasty retreat out the door and away.

Merle

by Rachel Burden

"Fire! Fire!" A cry guaranteed to chill blood in any Aroostook blood stream, but especially if you're crippled by polio, if it's midnight, if you're alone, if you're in your winter union suit (your only pajamas), if you're too sleepy to know directions, if you're just plain scared.

"Don't try the stairs, Mr. Higgins. I think they're on fire already, down lower. Let's try the window."

"The window!? That's crazy; How far down is the ladder?"

Several firemen were urging speed and trying to sound calm, failing to tell Merle the ladder was five feet from the opening. "You can do it, Mr. Higgins. We'll help you out, and then hold on. It's a safe drop."

"But I only have strength in one arm. Just take me back to the stairs!!"

"We'll all help. Let go. Wow! You did it!"

The scene was the old State Theatre, now known as the Braden Theatre. Because Merle worked at the bank, he was able to rent one of the third floor rooms. Heretofore the set-up had been great, free movies anytime you wish and close proximity to work. Such a bonus in winter.

Wrapped in a blanket, kind police took him to Mapleton, where anxious family awaited, praising God for his dramatic rescue.

<p style="text-align:center">~~~</p>

The Star-Herald reported the story in less personal terms on January 25, 1945:

The fire, labeled as one of the worst disasters of its kind in Aroostook County history, broke out shortly after midnight and gained headway from its point of origin, the State Theater.

Immediately after the alarm was rung in, night officer, Frank Giberson made his way up through the smoke filled lobby of the State Theater into the flame filled corridors of the third floor to awaken Mr. and Mrs. Hubert Hawksley and their three-year-old son Darrell who occupied the apartment on that floor. He also awakened Merle Higgins who occupied a room on the same floor. Giberson then proceeded to rap on the door of rooms used by two Bouchard sisters, Lillian and Rita, also rooms of Eva Clifford and Alice, but they were not in the building at the time. The Bouchard women rushed to the Hawksley apartment and then to Main Street in their night clothing. Then grabbing a blanket and wrapping it around his head, Giberson returned through the flames to the street. The blanket was burning briskly when he discarded it.

Hawksley picked up his young son from his cot and dashed through the flame infested corridors to the street below where Presque Isle firemen, aided by some civilians, were assembling ladders to reach Mrs. Hawksley and Merle Higgins, who were waiting above for ladder support. Hawksley was burned some around the face from his dash through the flames, while young Darrell's hair and eyelashes were singed. Firemen then removed Mrs. Hawksley to safety and then returned to rescue Higgins who had attempted to get through the flames.

By this time the firemen not engaged in rescue work, had assembled and connected hose to hydrants and were ready to concentrate on the job of extinguishing the blaze, which already had a sweeping start when they arrived at the scene. By the time Mrs. Hawksley and Higgins were rescued and the firemen had made sure that no other occupants were in the building to their knowledge, the front windows of the structure on the State Street side were livid with flames and the roof was shooting sparks at a merry pace. Handicapped by sub-zero weather, chief Leon Dorr and assistant chief, Hebert Treffery and their men worked briskly in the painful cold in the arduous task of checking the fierce onslaught of the galloping flames.

My Mother Told Us Stories
by Maxine Smith

A storyteller in every family would be nice;
    My mother was one. She told stories about earlier days,
Recited ballads and poems she had learned as a girl.
    Talked about neighbors and close friends of her youth;
Quoted proverbs and old sayings. She liked Shakespeare:
    "Something is rotten in the State of Denmark,"
She'd quote when doubting someone, or when suspicion rose.

She told those stories well, about her life as she grew up
    In old Masardis town. To us those days seem far away.
Parents seemed to be ancient; but really, she was very young,
    even then. We listened and felt we knew them well,
The ones she named: girlfriends Mabel, and Lettie, and Pearl—
    Older neighbors, Annie Pollard and great old Mrs. Hasson—
Names that even now seem familiar, like good friends remembered.
    It's like our lives entwined, although we never met.

She recalled a childhood filled with chores made fun.
    A berry picking race when all would vie
With pails tied around their waists to free up hands.
    "And did you always win?" we'd ask. Knowing well
Her answer would bring on another tale about the folks
    Who loathed to lose, but didn't always win.
We know about poor sports who pouted sad; no honor there—
    Her voice would lower as she shook her head.

One story made us hold our breath: She was thirteen, and
    With an abscess on her thumb. The doctor came to lance—

But gave her too much chloroform to make her sleep; And then
    He sighed, and told Gram sadly that this girl was dead.
Gram didn't wait, but snatched her up and took her out.
    She tipped her head and hung her by her feet;
And that child gasped and lived! Gram breathed, "Thank God."
    And my mom smiled, as she recalled that joyous day.

She often quoted "Papa"—his words seemed sage to her.
    "The rule for living is so simple; if only folks would do
As we're told in the Golden Rule. What man could turn away
    If we all did to others as we would be done to?"
She told us that her father hated lies; said he'd prefer
    To know a thief 'cause he could lock his door.
"But," he said, "You can't defend yourself if he's a liar.
    And once he's told a lie, you know you cannot trust again."

In early days, peddlers traveled around, town to town;
    The train arrived and dropped one off, and then she walked,
Carrying bags of goods to sell. Calling as she came to doors,
    "Here's Annie Marble, with wares to sell and tales to tell."
On Velma's birthday she came by and learned that girl was eight;
    Annie dug deep within her bag and found a gift—a dish.
That lovely colored glass reminds me yet, and I am old—
    Of all those many tales our mother told.

THE MEMORABLE VISIT
by Leonard Hutchins

They were very important visitors, my mother-in-law and my brother-in-law. Mom was a soft-spoken, gentle soul who had helped my wife, Phyllis and me for years. Cloud was a member of our finest generation. He had recently done more than his share to win World War II.

Wife, Phyllis was an unusually good cook. Whatever she prepared for dinner would be good. However, what did I have to share with our guests? As if Mom had read my mind before she arrived, Mom said to me, "Leonard, I have wanted a ride in a canoe since I was a little girl. Do you have a canoe?"

I still remember the pleased smile on Mom's face.

"Leonard," Cloud said after Mom had her canoe ride, "I'll bet you can't find, on short notice like this, something I've wanted since I was a kid before the war."

"What's that?" I asked.

"Hazelnuts," he said.

I still remember the pleased smile on his face.

Memories of Dad and Mom
by Leila Day

One thing I have to say is that we had the best parents! Dad was such a hard worker. He worked on potato farms all his life. The first farm I remember was the Bean & Allen Farm on the Houlton Road. It was right across from where the State Farm is. They gave us a house because Dad was one of the main workers. Later on he worked for the State Farm and we had to move because, of course, they wanted that land to grow more potatoes.

One of the first memories I have is of Dad going into the grocery store and coming out with four ice cream cones. I'll never forget that feeling! Four ice cream cones for the four of us! Well of course, that was before Marcia and Charlene came along.

I wasn't the oldest. My older brother was Bob. He and his wife Mary were missionaries for a while. I was next, then Ruby was a year younger, and then Clayton was five years younger; Marcia was the next one, and Charlene was the youngest. She was only seven when Mom died.

I guess it feels like the biggest memory is of life after Mom died. She had cancer and was only 49 when she died. I had graduated when I was 17 and about a month later, in July, I started in as a telephone operator. I was 25 when Mom died and I took night shifts so Dad and I didn't have to have a babysitter for the youngest ones. Bob was already married and on his own.

Dad would come home from a long day on the farm and take over from me. I can't remember when I slept, but Dad did everything for the little kids, supper, dishes, homework, bedtime and all the rest. Sometimes he'd drive me to work but in good weather I walked the two miles. Sometimes it was dark. Later on I learned to drive.

When I first went to work, everything was the old way, you had to call an operator to place toll calls. But later they went to computers and that was even harder work, as far as I was concerned. I'd been out four months after I had bypass surgery at 59. The phone company made the transition while I was out, and it was very hard to get used to the new system, when all the other operators had already been trained on it. It was hard not to be the number one operator anymore.

But one thing Dad always said was, "You make sure you always work!" It would have been awfully easy to stay home when Charlene was young, but then I'd be on welfare today. So I worked. I can remember they used to say, "Well, you should have gone on welfare" (or whatever they called it back then), but Dad said "I'm gonna work. We're gonna take care of our own."

I'm awfully proud of that!

As far as I'm concerned I couldn't have had better parents. Dad lived to be 77 and I was always there. Ruby was a missionary too. Marcia didn't remain close as she grew up, but Charlene and I were there for Dad. And we've always been there for each other.

One of the happiest memories I have was going fishing on the Aroostook River with Dad. We didn't wade in the water, we just sat on the banks and we fished. I had my fishing pole and he had his. We just sat there and fished. When Mom was alive, Dad could go fishing whenever he wanted. But we sometimes could get a relative to stay with the younger kids after Mom died, so we could go fishing. But not very often.

My parents were Ross (Roscoe) and Mabel Coffin Day. Mom came up north from Freeport and married Dad. I was named after a "Leila" on my mother's side of the family. I'll tell you one thing, they didn't come any better than Mom and Dad!

Christmas Past
by William McConnell

The scene is a small Aroostook town in a winter in the early 20s; isolated by unplowed roads and dependent on the railroad and telephone for contact with the outside world. One's childhood conception of Santa and the rites of Christmas came from books, the Bible, and oral tradition; all this before TV, radio, and movies could replace the imagined with the commonplace.

Earlier in the season, the church ladies group would have sewn up 6 inch square draw-string bags, made of white mosquito netting; to be filled with a mixture of popcorn, hard candy, and peanuts in the shell. A 12 to 15 foot evergreen tree had been set up in the front of the church, double the size of any home tree and huge in a child's eyes. By today's standards it would be sparsely decorated, without lights, ornaments, or hanging glitter, relying on red and green paper rope, tinsel rope, and strands of threaded popcorn.

A pageant, based on the Nativity story, involving the children would be developed and rehearsed, with plenty of walk-on parts, and lots of white sheeting for the shepherds.

Christmas eve most of the town would be gathered at the church; there would be singing, prayer, the pageant, and somewhere along the most memorable part for a child of impressionable age. Outside the church would be heard the sound of sleigh bells, commands of "Whoa Donner, whoa Blitzen," much stamping of feet in the entry, and in the door walked Santa, dressed not in the now familiar red suit, but in a long fur coat as worn by teamsters in winter. With a big sack over his shoulder, Santa would "Ho, Ho, Ho" and "Merry Christmas" his way up the aisle to the tree, and find in his sack one of the candy bags for every child present.

Never mind that the next year the child could readily guess that Santa was in fact one of the town's young adult males; for this year and these few minutes, Santa was as real as he'd ever been imagined.

A Sense of Scents
by Rachel Burden

Every once in a while an odor wafts by my nose and begins to trigger a long forgotten part of my childhood. Perhaps one of the most potent of these memory inciters is connected with our old model T and a special gasoline smell. How exciting when Dad would back the magic chariot from the garage to the front lawn and announce, "This would be a great day for a picnic!"

There was a time of adjusting the levers for spark and gas just right while Dad would be cranking out in front of the car. Sometimes one of the boys would sit adjusting spark and gas, but more often Dad would leap back and forth from crank to front seat. When the engine finally caught and stayed running, Dad retrieved the crank and proudly popped into the driver's seat. He didn't have to call "all board" because all were already aboard and excited. That wonderful odor from the Ford engine promised a get-away to somewhere—destination not that important. If it was a picnic, the provisions including firewood, a fry pan, cold baked potatoes, a coffee pot (pail?) and maybe some steak. We usually had no definite spot in mind, but would ride around seeking out a special place.

Flat tires were the norm more than a rare occurrence. Patching materials and an air pump were used more often than a spare tire and Dad was so efficient that the flat seldom dampened spirits or delayed our trip for long. I was a real Jonah for my father as I would remember every spot where we had a flat tire and say, "Oh, we had a flat tire here once."

One of my most memorable rides in the Ford happened when I was three or four. We were returning from visiting the grandparents in Chapman. Mariam was in front in Mama's lap and Irwin and I were in the back seat. When it began to rain, he and I crouched by the doors to miss as much rain as possible. My door didn't latch properly and I tumbled out. It is such a vivid memory for me. I picked myself up and started running after the car and crying, "Wait, I don't know my way home." Hurt or not I don't remember, just the panic of fearing to be abandoned.

Back to some strong scent memories, I would have to include baking bread, doughnuts frying, wood fires being built. At Grammy Foss', it might be flowers, apples, gem muffins baking or a medley of BenGay and other potions. In remembering Grammy Higgins, the strongest scent would be peppermint as you entered her room. I loved the smell of her clean apron when she rocked me in her big chair in the kitchen. How about cranberries cooking, the laundry smell on Monday, the scents are coming faster than I can write. Does it all make sense?

FROZEN IN
by William McConnell

Round Pond normally stayed open during hunting season, and a small plane could ferry people in and out.

One November 11th long week-end, a foursome from the University came to camp for the week-end; my brother Peter, his current girlfriend, and another young couple. They had flown into Fish Lake in a larger plane and got out on the beach near the outlet. There was a couple of inches of snow; they walked the two miles through the woods to camp. Already at camp were Connie, a hunter, my brother Bob as his guide, and me as cook.

The pond had frozen over unusually early, and when we all were ready to leave at the end of the weekend, we would have to go up to Fish Lake to get plane rides. The camp woods-phone let us make arrangements with Portage to get us all out of the woods.

We loaded all our luggage on the camp sled and went up the tote-road to the big lake. We found that the north end of the lake that we had approached was also frozen in. We shored along to what is now called Moose Point to find open water and the planes that had assembled to take us to Portage. Connie was the first to board, annoyed that extra luggage was put in with him. I got in Clair Moreau's plane; it was equipped with plywood floats, an answer to the aluminum shortage during WWII. They were famous for taking on water and getting water-soaked. We made a couple of attempts to get up enough speed to take off, but with no success. Going back to the beach, I got in Dana McNally's plane and was flown to Portage. In the confusion and hurry, nothing was put in with me, and I lost touch with the goings on. After everyone had left, Dana West, owner of the camps, found on the beach my rifle, left behind and retrieved the next spring.

FAREWELL TO THE FARM
by Marilyn Hoyt Chase

There was a moment of silence in the small room of the bank. Eyes were averted in embarrassment or in sympathy. No one wanted to witness the anguish and sorrow that shook the gnarled body of the seventy-year-old farmer, as he signed the deed, which would give his land away. His farm, his birthright—it had been in his family almost 150 years. It had come to this, slowly, but inevitably. High taxes, poor crop prices, and the overriding fact that in the northern parts of Maine, the big farms are getting bigger, and the small farms are gradually disappearing.

How much land does a man need? We all know the answer to that. In this age of cremation and other funeral rites, a man doesn't need that much. My father didn't need much—only one hundred acres measured out of the 1840's wilderness by one of the first Hoyt settlers to Fort Fairfield, Simeon Hoyt. Father had only been a twenty-year-old agriculture student at the University of Maine, when the managing of the homestead farm passed on to him. A burden some would have called it. Not so to Carlton Hoyt. The rich farmland was his mistress, and no land ever had a more faithful lover.

It's a good thing to be a farmer—a dirt farmer. It is to know the beauty of the sunrise as well as the sunset. It is to know all the seasons intimately and play out the drama against each, extemporaneously, never rehearsed. It is to put both hands into the rich good earth and breathe its pungent "mushroomy" aroma. It is to be, in the most basic sense, a creator. It is to be proud. During the thirties and part of the forties, my father used a team of two horses to pull the farm machinery. His was a potato farm and the furrows were long and even. I can remember stopping in the '29 Chevy on our Sunday rides as we came to a high point in the road, overlooking one of his fields.

"Look at them," he would command. "Don't they look straight to you?"

"Straight?" I would swell with admiration. My father could plant the straightest rows in the county even at the ends, green and heavy with potato leaves. And clean! There were no weeds in his fields. All four of us children spent our summers hand hoeing and hand pulling the occasional spear of mustard or kale, not only from the potato fields, but from the grain fields as well. To this day, I have doubts about any farmer who allows these weeds to flower in his fields. Slack and slothful, I always suspect. Not a real farmer.

And then there was the yield in the fall. How many barrels per acre? We were Depression kids and went to the small country school in that part of town called Maple Grove. Perhaps we four children bragged a lot—maybe to the point of being insufferable, but we always knew that our father would have a higher yield per acre than anyone else's father.

"It's the best damn land in Aroostook County," he would say with pride.

But it was more than the fertility of the soil. It was a careful nurturing of it: the meticulous cutting of the seed, the countless sprayings during the hot summer, interspersed with loving care, much like the mother to the child or the nurse to the patient.

I can see him now, walking out through the field roads, checking for erosion or plant damage after a particularly devastating thunder shower. Was it my imagination or did, under his loving scrutiny, the rain-sodden plants quickly resume their original shape? Trailing along after him, I could hear his murmured, "Yes, sir, you're doing fine."

Was it to the plants or to the larger Sir up there over the rainbow? As I trotted behind him, I would mutter my own incantatory prayer after each passed inspection row, "Thank you, Sir."

Years later, when I went away to college and began to encounter a more sophisticated and sometimes snobbish character of our society, I would always respond with sincere pride when asked my father's occupation. "He's a farmer." I could have added, "He is a lover of the land." For in my mind the two will always be the same.

To be a farmer is to be patriotic. For sons of the earth, like my father, even the simple lyrics of the song, "My Country 'tis of Thee" can always strike a response, primordial deep.

> .... I love thy rocks and rills,
> Thy woods and templed hills:
> My heart with rapture thrills,
> Like that above.

Could anyone who has not lived close to the land feel the rapture invoked by such a love song?

The farmer is quick to rail against restrictions, unfair government regulations, the blundering of bureaucracy. Nothing is sacred as far as politics and politicians are concerned. The potato farmer has been called, "Independent as a hog on ice," and not without some justification.

However, in the higher sense of duty to one's country, they stand at the head of the line. One of my father's greatest regrets was that he was too young for World War I, and although not too old for World War II, he was needed at home to run the farm. His sense of feeding the hungry multitude was strong. He would rouse us out of bed during the summer mornings with: "Rise and Shine! Roll out for reveille!"

While most of our friends enjoyed a summer respite at a lake, we four children had to help "Feed the Russians." Labor was scarce, as all able-bodied young men had been drafted or enlisted. For five long hot summers, father rallied us—three young daughters (Carleen, Marilyn, Janice) and one son (Richard)—with his call to the fields. He had us convinced, that without our help, the European armies would starve and go down in defeat. I have yet to meet my first Russian, but I have always felt a certain benevolence toward them. After all, their starving bellies had been filled from our own blood, sweat and tears.

Some have called the farmer a gambler. Perhaps some are. True, about those who try it for a year or so—just to see if they can make some quick money. My father was not a gambler. One year he would make a profit, only to have to turn it back into the land the next. How long could the farm keep operating when potatoes cost $3.50 a barrel to raise, and the farmer could only sell them at $3.00 a barrel? Up and down his finances went.

In the mid-fifties, early frost hit the fields before the potatoes could be dug. My father tried to salvage them, but frost-nipped potatoes break down in storage. His did. He lost three- fourths of the crop. Six thousand barrels, which would have sold that year for five dollars a barrel. Worry and strain broke his health, and he awoke one morning to find himself paralyzed, the onset of a virulent attack of rheumatic fever.

An influential farmer, Tom Haughton, pleaded my father's case, and the bank withdrew its threat of foreclosure. Plagued with arthritis and Paget's disease, he worked harder than ever. The farm, once free and clear, was now heavily mortgaged. We children could not help him. By then we had all married, had families to support, children to educate. We watched his struggle, powerless to contribute that which he needed most—money.

I was not prepared for his telephone call in September, 1971. "Marilyn, the doctors are sending me down to the Maine Medical Center. They want to operate. They say I have…" He could not say cancer, but the doctors did. They rushed him through. He almost died on the operating table. The doctors were dismayed and puzzled. It was not cancer. "Tuberculosis, maybe… No, not that. Perhaps some rare type of lung disease, caused by using pesticides over the years…?" It was never diagnosed.

He slowly recovered. I began to resent that land, which had exacted so much suffering from him. As I sat by his bedside one beautiful October afternoon, I asked, "Are you sorry Dad … that you became a farmer?"

Unspoken were my thoughts: Here you are at the end of your working years—years in which you've worked like a slave—and you've nothing to show for it but a mortgaged farm and a sick and hurting body.

He didn't even consider my question, but replied quietly, "I've never been sorry, NEVER. Not for one damn minute."

The land was his for yet a short while. That same fall, his son, Richard, in a financial sacrifice, left his own job and returned to the farm to direct the harvesting of my father's crop. But it was only a matter of time. Taxes on farmland were high. My father's tired body could no longer endure the pounding of the machinery, the extremes of weather.

No matter that the land was to be sold to the sons of one of his friends. No matter that these sons would take good care of the land. He was in a frenzy of despair and grief. He was selling the birth-right of his children and grandchildren. He was not keeping faith with his forefathers, who had passed the land to him. He would stand by the potato house, looking out across his fields, talking to himself. It was like a scene from *The Good Earth*.

"If I sell the land, it is the end of this family. This land was our birthright—our blessing. My childrens' childrens' roots belong to this land. Because of me, one day they may even go hungry." He would bend and take a handful of rich soil while silent tears fell.

But it was done—in the small room at the bank. We tried to be philosophical. "You didn't own the land. The land owned you," I said. "You have been a slave to it all these years. Now you are free." He merely looked at me in bewilderment. His bondage had been a thing of joy, of pride. He still owned the house. My brother was given the little homestead and five acres. But there was no assuaging his sense of loss and failure. I grieved for him.

In July of 1976, my husband and I went home for a short visit. On the morning before the Fourth of July, I asked, "Aren't you going to the parade with us?"

He looked at me with surprise. "The hay has to be cut. You don't understand." Off he went to help the young new owners.

I didn't understand, until later, when after a heavy rain shower, I walked with him out to the fields—fields which were no longer his. And as of old, I heard his murmured, "Yes, sir, you're doing fine."

And then I understood. Regardless of deeds and legal hocus-pocus, the land would be his, because he was the land's, forever and always. His land, his love would endure even as he played out his final hours against it. He had not been beaten in the end. He had made his peace…

I made mine as I echoed, "Yes, sir, you're doing fine."

Note: Carlton Foster Hoyt died January 17, 1983, at age 75. In the 1990's Cavendish Farms bought the farmland from Houghton Farms, Inc. My husband and I lived in the big house from 1988 to 2002. We sold the property to Dr. and Mrs. Thomas Hanf. Carlton's grandson, Richard Hoyt IV, lives with his family in the 1840's homestead as of 2008.

Grammy Dixon

by Phyllis Hutchins

My great-grandmother, Amelia Gallagher Dixon was the only grandparent I knew. She was a warm, friendly glow in my Great Depression childhood, and a solid anchor in crisis. During her visits to our New Brunswick farm just across the border from Fort Fairfield, her always soft-spoken evening stories were radio and television for us eight children. We listened quietly as we crowded around her rocking chair in front of our huge wood-burning kitchen stove. A small woman, she always wore an apron over ankle-length black dresses, usually a cameo pin at her neck, low black shoes, and her hair pulled close to her head and pinned in a bun behind.

In late years, when recalling those delightful evenings, I remembered that my hard-working mother was at the bathtub-sized kitchen sink washing the day's kitchen and dining dishes as well as dozens of steel cream separator parts. Probably, I think, Grammy Dixon told us stories in the evening to occupy us while mother worked.

While she told stories, Grammy smoked a clay pipe, holding it by a small tip molded under the bowl. She kept the stove ash drawer pulled out, and she occasionally leaned forward to spit in the ashes. This obviously annoyed Mother to no end, but Mother never complained. Mother loved Grammy Dixon, and she was, no doubt, delighted to have her brood quiet for a while.

Recently, a relative recalled that when Grammy didn't want someone or other to see her smoking she hid her pipe under her apron. Several of her aprons had holes scorched into them.

Over the years, I had a family and watched my children become part of extended families. With that experience, I added my memories of Grammy Dixon to events recalled by my extended family. Only then did I realize that my great-grandmother was a powerful adhesive that combined families into communities.

Grammy was born in December, 1849 at a place that would be called Limestone Siding, New Brunswick, years later when the railroad was built (a few miles east of Limestone, Maine). As a tiny, premature baby she was wrapped in sheep's wool to retain her body heat in the drafty house. With infant deaths so common at the time, it is perhaps miraculous that such a weak child survived. She remained a small person, but she became durable indeed. She married James Dixon, mothered thirteen children, and outlived all but two of them. When a daughter-in-law died, Grammy brought up seven grandchildren.

Grammy was an intelligent, sensitive, caring person who used her personal experience to help others. She became both midwife and undertaker for the community along the St. John River as far as a horse and wagon, the railroad, and in later years motor vehicles could carry her. Young mothers were more anxious for Grammy Dixon to arrive on time then the doctor. She often treated cuts, bruises, fevers, diseases, and whatever else might have been the problem. Perhaps her most valuable asset as a medical practitioner and undertaker was her soft, comforting voice.

Such was the case when my older brother died in 1939 of a ruptured appendix. Always moving as I remember her, Grammy comforted my family and coordinated our neighbors who came to visit, comfort, and help us. Most of all in that crisis, I remember Grammy's soft voice.

We moved to Fort Fairfield after my brother's death, and Grammy occasionally visited us. When she died in 1945, I felt deep, empty, loss.

Over the years, Grammy Dixon was always mentioned whenever the family gathered. We thought that our memories were all that we would ever have to remember Grammy. However, during the 1990's some of the family decided to build on to Grammy's old house. Photograph negatives were found. Surely, it was guessed, after all the years no pictures could be developed. Still, it wouldn't cost much to try. Coveted pictures of Grammy Dixon were distributed among her extended families.

Extended indeed. The names of Grammy Dixon's direct descendants and in-laws read like Maine and New Brunswick telephone directories. In addition to pages of Dixons and Gallaghers, the list includes Everet, Bradstreet, Fitzherbert, Norsworthy, Merrit, Jensen, Dale, Kelly, Redgate, Russell, Schwartz, Hall, Adams, Morrell, Staton, Cyr, Michaud, Hutchins, Pelkey, Christian, Flannery, Emery, and Sullivan. No doubt, I missed some of my cousins. There are great- and great-great-grandchildren living in the Portland area.

I am proud to be part of such a great lady's family.

FIRE THREAT
by William McConnell

Fire was always a threat to the substandard housing of the town of Portage, mostly heated with wood stoves. My mother got me up early one summer morning and we watched from an upstairs window as the sawmill started to burn. Later in the day I went down near the fire, which by then was most active in the area where the reserve boardpiles were burning, and where some boxcars also were lost. There may have been a breeze in from the lake; I was impressed by the glare and the roaring sound of the fire. The mill was rebuilt just in time to be caught by the first effects of the Depression of the early thirties, and soon shut down for good.

Sometime in the middle twenties Coffin's general store burned. Men in the area moved out much of the merchandise and fixtures, much of it scattered around on lawns out of the reach of the fire. The candy showcase was temptingly sitting far enough away from the excitement, and some of us filched a piece of candy; my choice, of all things, was what we called a jaw-breaker, hard candy nearly the size of a golf ball, that I sucked on for a while and then spit out. The store was rebuilt and still operates.

While I was away, Tanguay's Hotel burned. The story was told that Zeph Alward, who loved a drink, put a wet handkerchief over his face, crawled into the bar on all fours, reached up in the darkness, felt for a couple of bottles, emerged outside to the cheers of bystanders, to find that he had rescued two bottles of cleaning supplies.

While I was in Portage High School, near the end of the term, a fire started just toward town from the sawmill, possibly in the blacksmith's shop. It jumped from one building to another, and eventually burned most of the buildings that had belonged to the Mill Company. There was no fire department in town; the Maine Fire Department had a portable high-pressure pump and hose they could have set up at the lakeshore, but Brick, the Chief Warden, was out of town, and the equipment unavailable. As we watched from the third floor school windows, a stiff breeze off the lake blew a large cinder from the blazing buildings for some distance to land on the Hersey house that was quickly ablaze. We were let out of school early; fire equipment arrived from Ashland, but by that time all the buildings clustered in the path of the prevailing breeze off the lake had already burned, a dozen at least. Left standing by itself was the mill, eventually dismantled for its machinery.

By the time the George Sutherland house caught fire, the town had acquired a miniature fire engine based on a Jeep chassis. I was not present, but rumor has it that Mrs. Denny Boucher remarked that she could pee a bigger stream than the firemen were putting on the fire.

Motel 6—Where Are You?
by Rachel Burden

In the latter part of the 1920's, many Mainers joined the new craze—buying a car. Now, where to go? Summer meant dried country roads and vacation time. Vacation for most everyone, except for the busy Aroostook farmer; his life was busier than ever.

"Where shall we go? Our Higgins cousins will surely be home and we know they have lots to eat. There are potatoes and big gardens, so we won't cost them much. Besides we haven't seen Aunt Bertha for a few years. It's really our duty to make a call. She must be in her mid-eighties."

Unannounced, the Canadian car pulls into the Higgins dooryard. Gram's niece Josephine and son John, from Woodstock, are warmly welcomed by Hazel as she takes a brief respite from canning string beans. Gram is delighted. Josephine is such a favorite. Rachel and Mariam scurry down the field road to call to Dad, who makes time from spraying to greet the cousins.

This is not an isolated story. Every summer was time to travel, picnic, and catch up on visiting relatives. At the Higgins home, the boys (only three of them, now that Wallace was married), had moved out to the tent in the yard, leaving one empty bedroom upstairs. Before summer's end, that room might house Uncle Wren Cheney (great-uncle for four of Jennie's kids), Uncle Jonas, Uncle Charlie Smith (Gram's brothers), Lee Sherrard (cousin on Dad's side), Bessie Swayze, George and Georgie (cousins of Hazel) and many more. All were warmly welcomed and *knew* it.

Some of the stories told and retold over the years give you a picture of how the relatives expect such easy hospitality. For example, let me tell you of our Worcester aunt and uncle.

Grampy and Grammy Foss managed a small farm in Chapman beside Foss Brook. Other than hay for the cow and horse, Gramp raised a few potatoes, also a huge vegetable garden. Berries, apples, and trout from the brook augmented the diet. Summer was always a happy time. There was no refrigerator, but if you followed a path down to a spring house on the edge of the brook, there was always milk, cream, and butter. Oh yes, and fresh eggs from a small flock of laying hens.

Now you do want to know how they reacted to summer guests! Oldest child Lena (a step-daughter to Gram), had married a Massachusetts man and proudly birthed and raised four children. Every summer Uncle Eben brought his wife and four darlings by train to Chapman. After a few days, he was needed at his job and left. As he said good-bye to his wife and kids, his oft repeated words were something like this, "Now Lena, remember that this is your vacation. I don't want to hear that you are working hard on the farm. This is a time for you to relax and enjoy." Aunt Lena listened and nodded. She was a very wise daughter and mother. The parents *would* have help.

Uncle Eben was really a kind and very generous man. I imagine how he must have instructed his children on being helpers. Gramp was probably 75 or older at the time. When in later years, we quizzed Gram about this arrangement, her response was, "She's Llewellyn's only child from his first marriage. I'd do anything I could for her and him."

Jump to 25 years later, Freda and Hilston were owners of farm and house, one of our Worcester cousins had a restless son. "Could I send him up to you for the summer? I realize everything is free on the farm and maybe he could help you a bit."

Hilston was busy, busy with the irrigation on the farm. Freda was free from teaching, but deep into courses leading to her Master's degree and using her weekends to freeze and can from their bountiful garden. It seemed to be easy to say "no" to third cousins.

Motel 6 accommodations had changed remarkably in a few decades!

RAILROADS, THE GREAT DEPRESSION, AND BEYOND
by Roger Oakes

I was born, Elmer Roger Oakes, at Cottage Siding, St. Francis, Maine on November 19, 1924, the son of Herbie J. Oakes and Leanna (Daigle) Oakes. My grandparents were Charles Oakes and Anne (Bernier) Oakes and Edith (Nadeau) Daigle and Ovila Daigle. My sister, Micky, (Theresa B. Oakes LaPlante) was born October 17, 1926 and when I was thirteen, another sister, Jo (Mary Joan Oakes Villella) was born May 6, 1937.

At Baptism I was named Joseph Elmer Roger Oakes and a Franciscan Sister exclaimed with love, "We'll call him 'Roger," ending the short debate about naming me. My mother was agreeable, but my father wanted 'Elmer' to recognize a close friend instead of a relative. This interesting name allowed me to assume a number of aliases over the years. Roger Oakes, E. Roger Oakes, E.R. Oakes were the main ones.

My father was Station Agent and railroad telegrapher for Bangor & Aroostook Railroad in St. Francis. When an opening occurred for a station agent in Unity, Maine for the B&MLR (Belfast and Moosehead Lake Railroad) we moved there sometime between 1924 and 1925. The B&MLR ran from Belfast to Burnham Junction in the state of Maine. The railroad had stations in Belfast, Waldo, Swan Lake, Monroe, Brooks, Thorndike, and Burnham, where it turned around for the trip back. Winnecook had no regular station but the Unity work crew took care of the tracks to keep them safe for the trains.

I was fascinated by trains and used to visit the station in Unity to watch the trains come and go. One bad feature of watching the trains was the soot. The soot carried many grains of spent coal. These were apt to get in the eyes and made tears flow.

During the late 1920s the railroad sponsored excursions to Bangor, Portland, Lewiston, etc. on their return. They stopped in Unity anytime between the hours of 10:00 and midnight.

Because Dad was the telegrapher, he had to be on duty from 5:00 AM until the excursion train stopped in Unity to discharge the "revellers!" During this period Dad worked until 11:00 PM to 1:00 AM, whenever the train came through. This made for a long, long work day. Becoming overtired from the long hours with no break in the action, Dad resigned during the summer of 1929.

For a change in interest and employment Dad built a building to house a garage. The garage was finished sometime late in summer or early fall. Dad was no mechanic so he hired his youngest brother, Earl Oakes from St. John, in the northern part of the state. His qualification was: 1) He was out of work; 2) he was living at home; 3) he would take odd jobs—any work would do; 4) he was paying board to his parents, Charles and Anne (or Annie) Oakes, in accordance to what he earned, therefore it varied from month to month. Uncle Earl was young and a jack-of-all-trades.

The Depression hit October 1929 and Dad was caught without a job. Jobs were just not available. The economic times were "hard." Herbert Hoover was the president of the United States. It was unemployment for my father.

There were no savings as any money available went into the building of the garage. The garage operated with the meager money available. Dad then became the sole proprietor of one struggling business. Since he was not skilled in auto mechanics, about all he could do was change oil, add oil when needed, and grease the auto. He used a hand grease-gun that held a couple pounds of grease—enough to grease an auto or truck.

In a short time, it became apparent that Dad was unable, economically, to run a garage. He hired help, but no one stayed for more than a few days. When work was done, a paid bill was expected— BUT—Money was scarce. Unemployment was the order of the day.

Farmers used to run a tab for work done during the growing season. At a dollar a day workmen found it hard to get laborer pay.

Salaried people found their pay stopped and were then paid by the day. A day's work lasted twelve hours. Still, some couldn't get paid at the end of a day. Some were paid by check, but if so, usually at week's end—usually Saturday. MONEY WAS SCARCE!

I really don't know how Dad kept going. But somehow, the family survived. Being only five years old, my memories are mostly of stories told about that time.

～～～

Of all my aliases, Elmer R. Oakes was the name used by the selective service when I registered December 28, 1942. I was drafted April 14, 1943, and active duty began for me on April 21, 1943. I guess my skills in accounting and bookkeeping were recognized by Uncle Sam, because I found myself stationed in Tampa, Florida as a classification specialist. It was my job to analyze the strengths of enlisted men and determine their likely specialty. During those thirty-three months, I interviewed at least 3,000 men. I received an honorable discharge February 17, 1946 with the rank of Staff Sergeant.

I attended the University of Maine at Orono where I was the baseball manager and belonged to Phi Mu Delta Fraternity. There were fifty-five members, thirty-five of whom lived in the frat house. Of these members, all thirty-five of us earned letters.

I married the love of my life, Geraldine Keenan, on September 4, 1948 at St. Joseph's in Mars Hill by Fr. Adrian Palardy. I graduated with a degree in business administration in 1949. Around that time I worked in Boston, New York, and Orono and earned about $175/month.

I came up to Aroostook County to make my fortune—picking potatoes. I could pick thirty-seven barrels in one day! In November, 1949 when all the potatoes were in, I was hired by the IRS where I worked until retirement.

BAKED BEANS
by Phyllis Hutchins

Adam and Eve ate apples in the garden, but after they left, I'll bet they ate baked beans. Baked beans have been around that long.

I learned about beans, from beginning to end, during the Great Depression years. On our farm, we had what I remember as a huge bean field. After my father fertilized the land with animal manure, plowed and harrowed it, he used a piece of horse-drawn farming equipment to make straight rows. With the hoe handle, he punched holes in the loose soil a few inches apart.

As we eight children became old enough to count to four, we were taught to drop beans into the holes. My brother and I counted, "One for you, and one for me. One for the crow, and one to grow." I can remember how the cool, soft earth felt under my bare feet.

As the plants grew, father hoed earth up around them with horse-drawn equipment and the hand hoe. Since we youngsters were old enough to count, we were also old enough to tell bean plants from weeds, and pull weeds—all of them. Just before the first frost, the bean plants were as high as our waist and heavy with pods.

As frost killed the plants, the beans dried in their tough, shrunken pods. My father and older brothers stuck four- or five-foot sticks up here and there in the bean field. They pulled each hill of tangled dry bean plants and packed them, roots up, onto the sticks to dry better. The columns of bean plants on the sticks were big enough for us to hide behind when we played hide and seek. The sticks of beans were taken to the barn where they further dried to crispness.

Father and brothers laid the bean plants on the barn floor, one stick at a time, and flailed the beans from the plants. A bean flail is about a four-foot stick to which is tied a two-foot stick. The long end is grasped and the short end is swung to strike the plants. We youngsters didn't stand close. Both the flail and the flail-driven dry beans were dangerous.

The bean machine was a wonder to watch. The beans and small broken plant pieces were shoveled onto a screen. When father turned a crank, the screen shook and a fan spun. Beans dropped into a bag, and the chaff was blown away. Marvelous!

We must have used several hundred pounds of beans per year. In addition to our family of ten, we always had company, especially on weekends. Also during the Great Depression years, hobos came and went. They were not bums or tramps. They were good men who couldn't find work, but kept looking. My mother never refused them a meal.

Everyone ate beans. Mother baked beans in covered earthenware or cast iron pots every Wednesday and Saturday. She kept them warm on the back of our wood-fired cook stove, so beans were always ready to spoon from pot to plate and eat. We learned early on that we were not to eat from the spoon in the bean pot.

We grew yellow eye beans. The first step in the bean-baking process was picking out discolored beans and tiny rocks, which fell through the bean screen. Today I also bake smaller pea beans. When beans come in a neat cellophane bag, there are far fewer pick outs. However, from habit, I pick over the four cups of dry beans I need for a "batch."

Soak the beans overnight in a bowl large enough so the beans are covered by two or three inches of water. They soak up a lot of water, and it takes time. Next, drain and rinse the beans. In a six- to eight-quart bean pot or casserole, place two peeled onion halves, and pour in the beans.

I recall, with great regret, the next step in the bean-baking process— putting a half-pound of salt pork on the beans. That really made the batch. However, cholesterol, high blood pressure, and no-excuses diet came with my old age. Does that sound familiar? At any rate, I now use as much of a one-quarter pound stick of oleo as I dare. Since I can't eat very many beans at a time anymore, I also add two slices of bacon, just so I can remember what good salt pork on beans used to taste like.

Okay, enough of this whining about getting old. Next step, in a more or less two-quart bowl, put in three-quarter cup of molasses, two teaspoons of salt, two teaspoons of dry mustard and one-half teaspoon of chili powder. Fill with boiling water, stir well, and pour it onto the beans. Add enough boiling water to cover the beans.

Cover the pot or casserole, and bake it in a three hundred fifty degree oven for two hours. Reduce the heat to three hundred twenty-five degrees and bake for another three or four hours. Check frequently and add water as necessary to keep the beans covered. Try the beans to see when they are done.

The top beans, what is left of the two slices of bacon, and the two onion halves, which work their way to the top during cooking, are the best of the batch. Put this aside for a delightful cook's snack. No doubt, there will be too many beans for one meal. They last well in the refrigerator, and they freeze well. Enjoy.

Cherished Close Encounters with Father
by Rachel Burden

Rachel Burden is a published author with several local history books to her credit. The following excerpts are taken from a book written about her father, but, in her words, "not meant to be a biography." For those readers who can trace their heritage to the Higgins line, I urge you to devote some time to the Maine Genealogy section at the Mark and Emily Turner Memorial Library. Thanks to Rachel Burden, a forward-thinking woman of the 21st century, your heritage has been preserved.

Rachel Begins:

After my mother's death in 1978, I spent many hours with my father. Often we lingered at the breakfast table chatting about the weather, politics, world news, family news or sometimes, just sharing memories. When the memories began to slide into events of the past beyond my recall, I quietly reached for my notebook and became more of an interrogator than a conversationalist. Only once did Dad offer any objections to my scribbling. "I hope you're not writing that down. I don't want anyone to know that you had foolish ancestors."

I cherish those close encounters with my father. In our growing up years, there was always so much work to be done and so many of us in the family, that it was rare for any one child to have much private time with Dad. The purpose of my writing is to share with my sisters, brothers, children, grandchildren and cousins some of these glimpses back into our rich heritage. The fact that Dad was in his 90s when most of this material was jotted down, should not detract from the validity of details. His mind was keen and his ability to remember dates, prices and numbers was phenomenal.

Animal Tales, Ray Higgins-style

I once bought a riding horse at an auction in Presque Isle. Her name was Dixie. She was a pretty, high-spirited horse but I was certainly a mighty poor judge of ladies this time. No one mentioned to me the fact that she had never been properly broken. Life with her was a series of tantrums, contrariness, broken pungs and wagons, battered stalls and running away. Finally I bargained with a fellow uptown (let's just call him Sam) who said that he'd give me $40 for my horse. He really was in need of a horse and I tried to make a fair bargain.

After trying out Dixie, he changed his mind about the $40 and offered me a yearling heifer instead. I figured the heifer was worth about $20 but I agreed anyway. Later Sam came, saying that the horse was really too wild for him and he didn't feel he could give up his heifer. How about trading for a turkey? At this point, I let him take Dixie home and agreed to swap for the turkey.

Dixie proceeded to run away time and again and to cause Sam all kinds of grief. One day he appeared and reported, "I just can't let you have that turkey. He's a special pet of my wife. Would you settle for a rooster?"

"Sure, sure," I laughed in agreement.

The relief of not having Dixie really seemed like pay enough. It was enough! I never did see the rooster.

It would take a long time to tell about all the good horses we had. One special favorite was named Jack. What a great horse he was! If we had been out at night and started home, there was no driving needed. We let the rains fall slack and old Jack would take us safely right to the barn door.

Bill was another great driving horse. Once when your mother was driving Bill, he became spooked about something and moved fast enough to spill her out in a snowbank. She wasn't a bit mad at Bill, just at the husband who showed very poor judgment by laughing hilariously.

When Wallace was in college, potatoes were mighty cheap and I was afraid that I couldn't pay his bills. I decided to cut some wood and sell it to get his tuition money. I got up at four A.M. so that I could get two loads a day. Dime and Prince were not a matched team as far as color went, but they worked together beautifully. After I had cut the logs, I timed myself to see how long it would take me to load them on the bob-sled. One load took me sixty-one minutes. Dime and Prince had long legs and, even though the snow was deep, they could travel easily. They were great horses.

Swimming

Once Orin and Horace made a canoe out of a big pine tree. They worked mighty hard digging out that wood and finishing it, even though pine is a soft wood. I was invited to go for a ride with them and we just got nicely settled when the darn thing rolled over and we were in the water. Luckily I could swim.

(Where did you learn to swim, Dad? Were you just a kid?)

The mill pond up in Mapleton was a great place to swim and we young boys were always there in hot weather. I imagine that's where I learned to swim and I must've been young because it seems as though I could always swim. We had a nice deep hole behind some alder bushes up the stream where there was a real drop-off. One day a fellow was with us (it may have been Will Cook) and he couldn't swim. We didn't realize this until just as we were about to leave and we saw him floundering in deep water. Burchard gave a whoop, swam out and pulled him in.

One of the leading ladies of the town thought it was scandalous that the boys swam in the nude. She knew that it was true because she had been watching them with her telescope!

Buildings and Roads

The first building in Mapleton village was built on the spot where the Methodist parsonage is now. It was a log house put together with wooden pegs. The State Road was built quite a while before our road and it was natural for that to be the place where the first building began, at the junction of the Hughes Road and the road to Balls Mills. Our Mapleton Road was fine as a winter road, but, because of the swamp, was almost impassable other times of the year. Mother went to town once in a dump cart and when they came to the swamp, it was so muddy, they had to turn back, cross over the ridge and go to town by State road. Spring and fall, the horses were ankle deep in mud—splat, splat!

First the swamp road was simply a corduroy one. Gradually the corduroy logs were supported by layers of rock. Frank Winslow was one of the greatest workers in building the road. He and Will Winslow sold white flat rocks to people in town who put them under the sills of their new houses. These made an even, perfect surface for the sills. He got $.75 or sometimes $1.00 per load. In winter he'd rig up and keep hauling, only this time it was wood. Wood at $4.00 a cord—cut, slabbed, sawed and delivered was pretty small pay, but those men saved money and were considered pretty well off by their fellow townsmen.

Grandfather Charles built his first house down by the elm tree (rock pile) because there was a good spring there. Burchard told me that he could remember when the house burned. He pulled Grandmother Ruth out a window and saved her life.

The next house was built on the very site where we are now. The saw mill was running and lumber was plentiful. Two carpenters, Stewart and Morton, who owned the saw mill, brought down the lumber and their entire crew. Before nightfall the house was framed and shingled, finished enough so that the family slept there that cold March night. Uncle Horace wrote, "I helped haul logs for the new house to the mill with ox and cow pulling a single sled."

At this time we were living in a poor little frame house which my father had built on the spot where Weldon McPherson now lives. When I was about 16 years old, (1898) that house burned. I remember waking up in the middle of the night to the sound of breaking glass. Uncle Joshua, who was visiting us at the time, used part of the iron bedstead to break the window. Then he, Horace, Willie and I jumped out into the snow. We always wore our long-legged underwear and stockings to bed because the chambers were so cold. We moved in with my grandparents then. Wood burning stoves caused many homes to burn. This house was the one I brought Jennie into as a bride but, by that time, my grandfather had died. [Photos are included in the original family history edition previously mentioned.]

We lost this house in 1909. Priscilla and Wallace were just little then. The children were brought out of the fire safely, but Wallace hid behind the woodpile and no one could find him. The whole family was panicky and I can still remember that awful scared feeling in the pit of my stomach.

The fire started from brush that was burning down back. It was very, very dry everywhere and the fire followed the fence line up to the house. The wind was blowing fiercely. We went out to fight the fire, looked back and noticed that the fire had blown to the tinder dry shingles on our roof.

The day was Memorial Day. Uncle Orrin was in charge of a big celebration in Mapleton. A speaker had been engaged and we were all planning to go. Visitors coming up the road for the celebration stopped and helped us fight the fire. Jennie carried the broom outside and declared that at least she'd have a broom when they moved into the next house. Then she carried the broom back inside, left it and rescued something else. I used to keep some money in a little box upstairs. When we cleaned the ashes out of the cellar, I was quite surprised to find a little pile of nickels—quite usable.

That same dry May, a big fire swept up the Westfield Road and into Presque Isle. That was the time that Lu Keirstead lost her home on Allen Street.

When we rebuilt, it was a large square house that you children grew up in. One summer when Grampy Cheney was visiting us, he helped me build the kitchen, shed, garage addition that attached to the barn.

When we lost that house in 1949 all I could think of was all that good seasoned hardwood in the cellar, all gone! I had paid stumpage in

Duntown and with a hired man had cut, sawed, loaded, unloaded and stacked it in the cellar. We yarded it with horses (Roope helped me) and sometimes we slept in a woods camp rather than coming clear home at night.

Two Lessons from the Farm
words of Irwin R. Higgins (1919-1995)
shared by his sister, Rachel Burden

Rock Picking

One day Claude, Wallace and I took the horses and wagons and were picking rocks. Claude was picking on the left and driving the horses. Wallace was on the right and I was picking behind. There was a great big rock up ahead and it was on Claude's side. Since he was driving, he gradually swung the horses to the left, so by the time we got to the rock, it was on Wallace's side. Wallace saw what was going on and he proceeded to pick up the rock, but it didn't budge. Then Claude saw a chance to show up his brother, so he walked around the wagon and gave the rock a try. It was a really big one, and he got it only about 3 inches off the ground. Immediately Wallace pushed Claude aside, picked up the rock and threw it on the wagon.

I've thought about this incident a thousand times. Did the rock get lighter? Did Wallace get stronger? No, it was all in his head. He couldn't pick it up because he thought he couldn't! When it was revealed to him that it was liftable, then he knew he could. How many times since then I have run into impossible situations. Is a problem unsolvable because it can't be done, or because you have a narrow minded, limited view of the situation?

What narrow, limited lives we lead! Who is it that is holding us down, some force outside us or restrictions we place upon ourselves?

Barn Raising

One morning Dad said, "Today we are going to a barn raising for Bennie Hughes. In those days when a farmer wanted to build a barn he hired a carpenter. The carpenter laid out the timbers and frame work in a certain pattern on the ground. Just for a short time a lot of manpower is needed—about fifteen or twenty men. About four men would lift a beam, then about four more to pull with ropes, while several more push with long spiked poles. Each part of the frame is thus pulled into place and fastened. The barn isn't complete, but the framework and a good part of the first layer of siding is nailed into place....

While the men were working, the women were spreading cloths on tables in the yard and piling up dishes of the most delicious odors in the world—baked beans, homemade bread from homegrown wheat, apple pies, baked potatoes, home raised vegetables and homemade ice cream.

How could anything be more wonderful! It was a sunny, clear day with a gentle breeze. Across the road there was an eighty-acre field of rich green potatoes. On the other side of the road was a golden field of oats ready for harvest. Everyone was kidding, joking and laughing heartily. Then it hit me! This is perfection! These people have created a little heaven here. A hundred years ago our ancestors came thrashing through the woods. They cleared the land, built cabins and houses, barns and churches. They worked hard and fought disease, death, cold weather and all kinds of obstacles. And they came out on top laughing. Yes Sir! There is no picture of heaven any more wonderful or beautiful than a barn raising!

BUILDING NEW MEMORIES
IN THESE
Golden Years

GREAT MEMORIES, GREAT PEOPLE
OF THE MAINE FOREST SERVICE
by Leonard Hutchins

It was just a little whiff of smoke back then. It was just a little whiff of smoke recently that reminded me of that day back then.

My work partner, Terri, and I listened to the Maine Forest Service radio as we repaired and painted a Forest Service camp near the Québec border. It was a blue sky morning, but there had been a dry thunder and lightning storm the previous night. Terri and I could change jobs immediately if someone saw smoke.

And someone did. The pilot of a pontoon-equipped plane carrying fishermen to a backwoods lake reported a small smoke on Bear Mountain down Eagle Lake from John's Bridge.

"Oh, no," Terri said. "That place is a mess. It was logged over and now it's covered by a deep mat of dead trees, limbs, and second growth. I really don't need to wade through that for a job today." She knew the area. She was one of the last fire tower operators.

"Be positive," I said. "Nobody can find a little smoke like that. It will burn out. As if in reply to my comment, a Forest Service ranger spoke over the radio network directing a Forest Service airplane to the approximate location and a boat to John's Bridge. Terri and I were directed to go to John's Bridge.

"Sorry about that 'be positive' comment," I said as we put our tools away. Terri rolled her eyes as women sometimes do when the occasion demands.

A boat, motor, fire tools, and a ranger were waiting for us at John's Bridge. We had an absolutely splendid ride up Eagle Lake to Bear Mountain. The airplane pilot gave our ranger a compass bearing to the smoke.

Just as Terri said, the route up Bear Mountain was indeed covered with a mat of dry, broken ankle-deep bushes, knee-deep saplings and very deep trees. It was a slow, laborious trip, sometimes walking over tree trunks several feet off the ground.

Suddenly, inexperienced as I was, the potential of the situation dawned on me. Somewhere up ahead was a small fire. If the wind shifted, the small fire could travel faster than we could through the dead mess. I kept sniffing for smoke.

The "fire" turned out to be little puffs of gray smoke rolling up from a lightning-shattered tree stump. We raked fuel away exposing a garden-sized, bare fire-proof spot, felled and cut the smoldering tree stump down, cut it into pieces, and covered it all with dirt. We won. The fire was out.

The hike back down Bear Mountain was easier than the hike up. We could avoid the worst of the dead mess because we didn't need to follow a compass bearing. The evening boat ride down Eagle Lake was more splendid than the morning ride. Sunsets on backwoods lakes are spectacular. I offered to drive Terri's pickup to our worksite but she would have none of that. "You'll hit a moose and I'll have a lot of paperwork," she explained. She might have been right. She had to avoid several moose on our way back.

One more thing: I wish I hadn't aged so soon. I'd still be working with the great people in the Maine Forest Service.

Spare Time
by Maxine Smith

My friend Barbara goes to the library each Friday after her hair appointment to pick up the numerous books that she has reserved for the coming week. I listen with envy as she tells me of the amount of reading that she does. She chooses books that are bestsellers and on reserve at the Library, and she goes religiously each week to replace them with more of the same. I listen as she details her pleasure when she read the latest, asking me if I have read any of that certain author's books. I usually haven't, and feel very humble as I admit that.

When I retired from teaching, I was sure that my days would be spent as hers are, just leisurely pouring through one book after another, getting to know all the great authors, and soaking up all that knowledge. Not so! I do well to read one book in a week, as I seem to have difficulty just sitting down to read when there are so many other ways to spend my time.

First, is my class in Body Recall, a very low impact exercise routine for keeping physically fit. This takes one hour three times a week, which we feel is reasonable, because who wants to chance arthritic pain as a companion in their declining years? On some of the days that these classes are held, I decide afterwards to visit one of my friends. Perhaps Mabel, who has had a bad winter with her broken wrist, and would appreciate a bowl of soup to heat up later for her lunch. Another friend works at City Hall and if she can arrange an early break, we may go for lunch at the Hotel, to let her get out of her office for a short reprieve.

On Wednesday mornings at 9:00, our Church Circle in Mapleton meets for Bible Study and a fellowship coffee. I do enjoy this class, and I benefit from the fellowship time. We are usually finished by noon, and I head for home to study my lesson for next week. At 2:00 that afternoon, I am scheduled to take my cousin Phyllis to physical therapy at the hospital. She crushed her left knee in a bad accident in October, and needs therapy three times a week. I don't resent the time used, as she is such an upbeat person, and we get a chance to visit on the way. While she is in therapy, I have three-quarters of an hour to visit friends there in the hospital or in the adjacent nursing home. If I would take my book along, I might read for that forty-five minutes, but on Wednesdays there are twin eight-year-old girls there for therapy due to borderline Cerebral Palsy. They always get my attention away from my story.

Rita Martin called, and needed someone to read to the residents at the Nursing Home, one afternoon a week. "Only one hour," she says, "on Fridays at 3:00 p.m." That seems rather easy, and I love to read, so I accept that challenge. Now, if only I can remember to be there and not schedule some other activity. I will write it on my calendar.

Our Church Administrative Council meets on the first Monday of the month, which is tonight. I have volunteered to furnish a worship service for the meeting, so I will spend part of this afternoon preparing the meditation. Many of the others hate to do this, but I find it rewarding, as I have to read quite a bit in devotional books and articles before I find just what I want to use for this time. Meanwhile, I learn a lot about myself as I read this type of literature, and I get to read aloud at the meeting, which I don't mind.

Weight Watchers is on Tuesday mornings at 9:30. I have been attending for twenty-odd years, and seem to find the sessions a big help in maintaining my weight, so the time I spend there seems worth it. That afternoon, I will attend my wonderful class in Creative Writing. Maybe Glenna Smith will assign a book for me to read. She may feel that we need examples of good literature spinning around in our heads before we undertake to write creatively.

My husband, who usually spends his days at work with our sons on the farm, said that he would like to find a day to go to Bangor to shop.

Thursday seems to be the one we can both get away, so we schedule that. I could read in the car on the way down, but that would seem to be telling him that I don't enjoy his conversation, so that is out. Earlier in my life, I was able to read in the evenings, as he watched TV, but now I can't seem to concentrate when I try to do that. Knitting makes it possible to stay in the same room, but I'm not getting that book read.

Our grandchildren love to sleep over, and often call to ask if they can come. We both do enjoy their company, and want them to have good memories, so some days my reading is in children's books read in the rocking chair. That is more fun anyway!

No, I am not getting all those "top ten" books read that I had planned. Some nights when sleep seems impossible, I do read and enjoy the solitude and quiet of the hour. Perhaps when I get really old, and have nothing to do, I will find the time to read all those bestsellers that I am missing today. In the meantime, I can just complain about my busy life and leave the books in the Library.

February 23, 1993

BINGO

by Leonard and Phyllis Hutchins

A lottery game was started in the 1500s by the Italian government to make tax money. It worked. Today it still contributes more than $75 million per year.

Over the years several game card arrangements have been designed to make money and teach subjects such as spelling and mathematics. Beans were used to cover the numbers on the cards, so the game was called BEANO.

In 1929 a game manufacturer saw a game, made a set of cards, bought some beans, and invited his friends to play. The game was a resounding success. A lady became so excited by a winning number that she jumped up and instead of shouting "BEANO" she stuttered "B-B-B-BINGO." She named the game we play today.

Phyllis:

Shortly after BEANO became BINGO, my family (six kids) moved to Fort Fairfield from Canada. Money in the Great Depression years was tight, but one year our mom and dad bought us one present, a BINGO game. Mom might have regretted that present.

Every night after supper we kids gathered with two kerosene lamps at our kitchen table to play BINGO. Little hands slapped the table. Big fists pounded. The lamps bounced. It was lucky that those lamps had big, heavy glass bases.

Wow. Hey, when did those years go by? Suddenly we were parents, and our kids played BINGO. Hey more years went by. We became grandparents, and our grandchildren played BINGO. Can this go on? Indeed it can. We found a retirement home. Guess what? We play BINGO.

Well, it wasn't quite that easy for me. Sometime during those years that flew by I acquired diabetes, and I neglected it. DON'T DO THAT! I lost my sight. I couldn't play BINGO with my new friends. The BINGO cards and the numbers were too small. So this is not a new thing. I can't read (Leonard reads for me) or watch a movie or television either.

However. Tina, our recreation director, came up with a humongous white BINGO card with equally big black numbers. Now I can play BINGO again, and listen to all the BINGO comments. Leonard collected a few for us.

1. A quarter is worth more when you win at BINGO.
2. How come the women win more often when Tina rolls the cage?
3. Only women can play four cards and keep up.
4. You need to be at least halfway smart to play more than one card.
5. If I don't win pretty soon, I'm going to play with pennies.
6. Hey. I just won enough to talk to a used car salesman.

7. Get your quarters ready!

8. Quiet down! We got a game goin' here.

9. Just leave your quarters on the table. Someone will pick them up.

10. Yeah. They sure will.

11. You won three straight. Lend me that card.

12. Look! I mean B4, the number. Not before, the word.

13. I've got to win enough to have my fingernails fixed.

14. Quiet! I can't win if I can't hear the number.

15. Of course I can use a ten for one. The zero doesn't have any value.

16. Has anyone ever won four cards at once?

17. Watch your own damn card!

18. Hey, what was the number, three numbers ago?

19. My fingernails are too short. I can't change the color.

20. If I pay more for a card, will I win more?

21. Wait. Wait. I've got to go to the bathroom.

22. Wait. I need time to complain.

23. Look. If I don't win, this game is rigged.

24. Hey! I can use 51 for 15 can't I?

25. Hey! Call my number. It won't cost you any more.

BINGO!

RECALLING THE CHURNING
by Rachel Burden

The starting point for my idea of describing churning from childhood memories was when my housekeeper said, "Churning? Never heard of that word before!"

Probing Village friends' memories has been rewarding, but there are still questions floating about. My imagination helped as I envisioned this little play:

Cast: Mama, Mariam, Grammy, The Boys (Claude, Irwin),
Ethel (Massachusetts cousin), Papa, Rachel

Place: Higgins Kitchen, AM (1930?)

RACHEL: Where's Ethel? She wanted to watch the churning process.

MARIAM: She's out in the barn, watching "the boys" finishing milking and doing chores. Our city cousin is eager to experience all she can in just two weeks.

RACHEL: I'll fetch her. The fun is about to begin.

MARIAM: Papa brought up from the cellar our big crock-full of sour cream. We'll dump it into the churn and take turns at the crank.

ETHEL: What are all those utensils in the sink?

MAMA: When the butter has, "come," I'll use that big oval tray and the wooden paddle to work and work the butter. When it begins to hold together, I'll use the wooden, rectangular device, which is guaranteed to form a pound at a time. The liquid from the churn is carefully drained off. See the little spigot. A favorite drink for Grammy and great for cooking is *butter milk*.

RACHEL: Next the special wrapping paper is laid out. It's a special type of paper, sized especially for our pound bricks, with a chance to write our name on the front.

MAMA: Ray will take this week's butter supply, along with our last churning, to the grocery store. Things like flour, peanut butter, coffee, tea and sugar are on my list. We won't be able to pay for them all this time, but we have good credit. Chances are there will be a steak, and also a few chocolates.

ETHEL: Thank you for letting me do some of the cranking this morning. Your butter-making tray is exactly like the ones Grammy Foss and Aunt Grace have. Where did they come from?

Wanting to accurately describe the brown wooden tray in which the butter was worked, I sought local help. Friends probed their memories, trying to help me out. Bill McConnell was especially helpful with vocabulary. Kathy, my daughter, searched the internet. Our library was visited. Oh such heavy books!

MAMA: I know exactly what you're describing, but I'm not sure of the wood used. They were hand-me-downs, found in most Aroostook County farms that kept cows. Some were circular, some were oblong.

From Ray Higgins: *His Mapleton Memories* by Rachel Higgins Burden, 1981:

"From 1919 until the early sixties, Dad kept his accounting recorded in books furnished by the Extension Service. As a record of the economics of Aroostook County over four decades, they are valuable to preserve and peruse.

"Very few of the early years of the thirties show accounts in the black at the end of the year. In 1931 the books did show a profit of $668.70. That same year, cream sales amounted to $848.36."

I'm including this quote so that readers will know that I'm not guessing at numbers and dates. The thirties were HARD Depression years.

Another quote from the "Ray" book:

From 1933 to 1939, eggs went as low as 20 cents a dozen and as high as 40 cents. Butter was as low as 25 cents and as high as 45 cents.

Lucky the families with cows and hens in those bitter years!

To close out this tale, which started with an excited churning in my ears, I'd like to share a wonderful quote from my Dad. I found it nestled in with some sorrowful Depression accounts.

A farmer should possess a sense of humor as large as a load of hay, a constitution made up of rubber shock absorbers and a disposition that responds to all the truth and beauty of country life.

—Ray Higgins

Hang In There!
by Phyllis Hutchins

At about age forty-nine (I'm eighty-six now.), diabetes descended upon me. "No big thing," I thought. "Pills controlled my father's diabetes. I can handle this."

Silly woman. Print slowly became blurry—even headlines. I had to borrow my husband's glasses to use with mine to set the knobs on my stove. "But new glasses will fix me right up, for sure."

When my optometrist friend looked into my eyes his smile dissolved. "You don't need glasses. Go see the ophthalmologist. Right now. This morning. I'll make your appointment. Now. He leafed through his phone book as I left.

Busy as he was, the ophthalmologist had a chair ready for me. "Some of your sight might be saved with laser surgery," he said as he prepared for my first of many appointments. Only then did I realize how silly this woman had been.

Life became complicated. Seven-year-old grandson, Alan, became my driving guide. He was good, and I drove slowly. No fender-benders.

But one day…"Watch out for the deer, Gram."

"Deer? What deer?" Whump! Poor deer.

"Gee, Gram. Didn't you see that deer?"

I didn't see that deer. I knew I wouldn't have seen a child, either.

Should I stop driving? I should…but that would be a very major inconvenience. "I'll drive slower," I decided.

On a trip later in my laser surgery career, what looked like a large piece of black road scurried into the woods. It had to have been a bear. There is nothing else that big, that fast, and that black in Aroostook County. Children sometimes wear dark clothing. I wouldn't have seen a child either, and children aren't as fast as bears. I might have hit a child. Again I wondered, "Must I give up the freedom of driving?"

Still later, on a shopping trip with my husband Leonard driving, he slowed the car, and I asked why.

"There is a fire truck parked up ahead," he said.

I looked ahead, squinted my eyes, and looked again. Sure enough. Huge, red, and with big yellow lights flashing, there was a fire truck parked by the side of the road. A fire truck! I couldn't see a humongous fire truck until we were passing it. And I couldn't see men in brilliant yellow coats until we drove past them.

That was my deciding instant. I might well have hit those men, or children, or mothers who might have been there. I haven't driven a car since. I was, and I am, proud of myself for doing the right thing—finally.

However, darkness gathered. I had no driving license, I couldn't knit, sew, read a newspaper or book, read radio dials, and TV zappers are impossible. I am pleased talking books work for some visually impaired friends, but they didn't work for me. Words like "dungeon," "mine," and "midnight" came to mind.

On the other hand, all was not lost. True, I couldn't read my recipes, but my husband likes to eat. He reads recipes, gathers ingredients, adjusts the stove, sets the table, makes coffee… oh, togetherness.

Sewing a quilt was out of the question for me, but Husband offered to cut material and sew the edges as needed so I could tack a child's or doll's blanket—my favorite hobby. There are so many beautiful children's patterns. The cloth feels like cloth, but it looks to me like shadows. But with long patience and much light the pattern appears on the shadow, sort of like seeing trees in very early morning twilight. Also, oversize measuring boards with oversize black measuring marks help me manage the shadows. A four-inch wide board with tacking marks every four inches gives me tacks every four inches for a child's blanket. Three-inch measuring boards give me tacks closer for a smaller doll crib blanket.

This does work, but, but, but… have you ever tried to teach a man to use a sewing machine?

So, I still have something useful to do for needy children, and there are a network of people in place to deliver my (our) work. A few years ago, Marden's needed thirty-five hundred children's blankets to send to Haiti. (I wonder if some of my work helped kids there.) United Way and Toys for Tots (USMC reserve) do this. Homeless shelters, police, fire fighters, churches, and hospitals deal with needy and sometimes terrified children.

If you join me we won't be alone. Check the "Linus Project" on a computer.

Thank you all.

Note: Our beloved Phyllis wrote this in 2014. She passed away October 13, 2015.

FAMILY REUNIONS
by Leonard Hutchins

When I was a Great Depression kid (and didn't know it), family reunions of a dozen or so at a lake were great. Mom's light-colored, short-sleeved dresses hung about halfway between her knees and ankles. Grandmother's ankle-length dresses with wrist-length sleeves were black with white cuffs and collar—always. Of course, they both wore cameo pins at the neck—always.

Once, I stood waist deep in the cold lake wearing swim trunks. I challenged my grandfather who was standing on the shore, dressed in his Sunday-best clothes, to come in and get me. My father and uncles sat dressed in their Sunday-best clothes, on the running board of a square-bodied car. They watched the event as they turned an ice cream freezer crank. Mom and Grandmother stood close to Grandfather.

Suddenly, Grandfather, experienced on log drives, accepted the challenge. Water splashed. Mom, Dad, and my uncles laughed. Grandmother scolded. I stopped laughing only for the few seconds I was dumped in that cold, cold lake. Good laughs are part of family reunions.

At lunchtime, a huge table cloth was spread on the lake shore. Folding furniture was set up for the grandparents. Sunday-best dishes and silverware were set. There were several kinds of salads and many kinds of sandwiches for lunch. And of course, cookies, cake, and ice cream. Because mom didn't want the tablecloth to get wet, I sat on a chair beside my wet grandfather. Could anything be better?

As it was supposed to be, that event was an opportunity to visit. It reunited the family.

～～～

In recent years, a family reunion of several hundred—at a lake, of course—was great. The women wore everything from slacks to shorts and granny dresses to miniskirts. It was a hot day, and T-shirts were the rule for all. Some of the youngsters didn't wear much at all.

Two dozen or so gas and charcoal grills were busy, and there was a restaurant and bar nearby. There were identifiable burgers, hot dogs, ribs, and sausages as well as all sorts of exotic stuff with exotic tastes. Paper and plastic plates, cups, and eating utensils were everywhere. Everyone, it seemed, had enough of everything. The restaurant and bar also did well.

The place was a friendly bedlam. Kids played games and swam. People in ever-changing groups talked. Young parents kept close track of young children. Used paper and plastic picnic ware was deposited in trash containers. New family members, the tiny ones and new in-laws from around the world (the ones who cooked the exotic stuff) were introduced with pride. When it became apparent that the teenagers had found some sauce, parents collected their driver's licenses and car keys. The only items on the agenda were, have fun and get acquainted.

One lady, reserved and quiet by nature, stood sweating in her granny dress. Suddenly, she lifted her dress to her waist and fanned her sweating legs with the folds of cloth. She received applause and laughter. She was also wearing a pair of quite-long denim shorts. Good laughs are part of family reunions.

As it was supposed to be, that event was an opportunity to visit. It reunited the family.

SEVENTY-ODD YEARS AND NO CHANGE
by Leonard Hutchins

It was a strange situation. Just a while back a group of young truckers told me the same thing that my first grade teacher, Miss Blanche Ginn, told me in 1936: "Leonard, you've got to pay attention!"

A senior neighbor had invited me to attend a two-evening Maine Driving Dynamics class given primarily for the young truckers. Speeding (more than once) had put the youngsters' licenses in jeopardy. Attending the class helps them to keep their licenses and their jobs.

They were a good-natured bunch. I had worked with one on a forest fire a few years back, and had another as a student more recently. My senior neighbor and I apparently looked out of place. The fellow I had worked with represented the class and asked, "What the hell are you guys doing here?"

It was fun to watch the expressions on their faces as my neighbor and I answered his question. We explained that our reaction times are slowing. We don't see or hear as well as we used to. We are more absent-minded than ever. On and on. We said that we were there just to remind ourselves of these things so we would be safer drivers.

What we said obviously didn't fit the young truckers' perception of seniors in general and senior drivers in particular. They didn't seem to think that we seniors could recognize our problems, let alone admit them. Bob Cormier, the course instructor and a senior himself, allowed time for discussion. I asked the youngsters for their opinion of senior drivers.

Remember, these young men work on the road, and they know what happens on the road. They are good at what they do, but occasionally they do it a little fast. The fellow who asked the first question asked,

"Do you really want the truth?" We assured them that we did and that I would include their views in this article.

They were polite but serious. Collectively they said, "You guys scare the hell out of us. You don't pay attention to traffic behind you. You stop right in the road anywhere you see something interesting. During the fall when the leaves change color, you are a serious road hazard. In some places, driving too slow is more dangerous than driving too fast. Our rigs and loads weigh up to 40 tons, and we need room to stop.

"You either don't use your signal lights at all, or you leave them on all the time. We are here in this class because we have to be responsible for what we do in our vehicles. If you can't be responsible too, you shouldn't be driving. You can't expect young drivers to bail you out every time you make a mistake." And more.

There was friendly banter. We seniors put out that we were in class voluntarily, but that the young truckers were there for speeding. They pointed out that the Maine State Police tend to be lenient with seniors but not with young truckers, that's for sure.

All in all, it was a good experience for both seniors and young truckers. We understood each other better. I think the young truckers would have been more favorably impressed with seniors if there had been more of us in the class. However, since neither the young truckers nor the Maine State Police are going to change anytime soon, there will be more such classes for us to attend.

For days after the class, I wondered about senior drivers. We're "slipping" we know, but are we all really such bad drivers as the young drivers thought? Everyday observations are one thing, but statistics offer another, and sometimes different, view. I decided to see some statistics. The Maine Department of Transportation referred me to the Office of the Secretary of State. They were generous with information—and sources for more information.

Statistics do, indeed, show a more detailed picture. In a recent year, there were 154,834 aged 65 and over Maine drivers. We made up 16% of the driving population and accounted for 16% of fatal vehicle crashes. Does that mean that we seniors can drive as well as experienced, young adult drivers? Well, some of us can. However, drivers over 75 had fatal vehicle crashes about as frequently as inexperienced 16 to 19-year-old drivers. So, some of us can't drive as well as experienced, young adult drivers. If this situation is part of a "second childhood" the Maine Legislature, I think, is right to enact age-specific laws (as they have done) to protect drivers and pedestrians from both childhoods.

It seems to me that the young truckers in the Maine Driving Dynamics class didn't distinguish between competent young seniors and less confident old seniors. But how could they? They haven't had experience to do that.

No doubt, some of my peers, old senior drivers, are not pleased with this point of view. Frankly, it scares me. Because of serious diabetes-caused eye problems, my wife is afraid to drive anymore. She did not renew her license. Cataracts were impairing my vision. Our home is well outside of town. If I, also, were to lose my ability to drive safely, it would be at least an inconvenience. Let's note, such an inconvenience is better by far than causing a fatal vehicle accident, particularly if it involved a young mother and children.

However, and note this carefully please, there is both hope and help for many senior drivers. For instance, a study showed that seniors who had eye surgery had a crash rate 50% lower than those who didn't have eye surgery. My eye surgery improved my sight much more than I hoped.

In another study, drivers who showed a 40% or greater impairment in their useful field of vision were more than twice as likely to be involved in a crash within three years of testing. But after ten computer training sessions on how to make quick decisions drivers can improve their performance by as much as 300%. Hope and help indeed.

There is more information and other programs available, too many to list in this article. In short, if we senior drivers do our part, we can drive safely longer. Also, my neighbor and I plan to attend another Maine Driver Dynamics class next year, just to keep driving safety in mind.

The fun of dealing with young truckers' points of view is a plus.

Sometimes we are so inspired by the work of like-minded writers that we can't help but leap from their shoulders into our own words. When this happens, a kind of magic flows over time, beyond earthly dimensions, as it did for our friend, Bill McConnell.

Birches
by Robert Frost 1874–1963

When I see birches bend to left and right
Across the lines of straighter darker trees,
I like to think some boy's been swinging them.
But swinging doesn't bend them down to stay
As ice-storms do. Often you must have seen them
Loaded with ice a sunny winter morning
After a rain. They click upon themselves
As the breeze rises, and turn many-colored
As the stir cracks and crazes their enamel.
Soon the sun's warmth makes them shed crystal shells
Shattering and avalanching on the snow-crust—
Such heaps of broken glass to sweep away
You'd think the inner dome of heaven had fallen.
They are dragged to the withered bracken by the load,
And they seem not to break; though once they are bowed
So low for long, they never right themselves:
You may see their trunks arching in the woods
Years afterwards, trailing their leaves on the ground

Like girls on hands and knees that throw their hair
Before them over their heads to dry in the sun.
But I was going to say when Truth broke in
With all her matter-of-fact about the ice-storm
I should prefer to have some boy bend them
As he went out and in to fetch the cows—
Some boy too far from town to learn baseball,
Whose only play was what he found himself,
Summer or winter, and could play alone.
One by one he subdued his father's trees
By riding them down over and over again
Until he took the stiffness out of them,
And not one but hung limp, not one was left
For him to conquer. He learned all there was
To learn about not launching out too soon
And so not carrying the tree away
Clear to the ground. He always kept his poise
To the top branches, climbing carefully
With the same pains you use to fill a cup
Up to the brim, and even above the brim.
Then he flung outward, feet first, with a swish,
Kicking his way down through the air to the ground.
So was I once myself a swinger of birches.
And so I dream of going back to be.
It's when I'm weary of considerations,
And life is too much like a pathless wood
Where your face burns and tickles with the cobwebs
Broken across it, and one eye is weeping
From a twig's having lashed across it open.
I'd like to get away from earth awhile
And then come back to it and begin over.
May no fate willfully misunderstand me
And half grant what I wish and snatch me away

Not to return. Earth's the right place for love:
I don't know where it's likely to go better.
I'd like to go by climbing a birch tree,
And climb black branches up a snow-white trunk
Toward heaven, till the tree could bear no more,
But dipped its top and set me down again.
That would be good both going and coming back.
One could do worse than be a swinger of birches.

BIRCHES

by William McConnell

I, too, have seen an ice-storm's beauty and tragedy
The bowed birches midst the wreckage
Of the proud, brittle poplars
That have lost their heads.
And I have been a swinger of trees,
Though not of birches, and never so often
The same tree swung as to leave it bowed.
And I have trod the "pathless wood,"
And face-felt cobwebs and the lashing twigs.
And who wouldn't leave a hum-drum now
To return to a new tomorrow.
But not too long and not too far.
For all its troubles, Earth's the place to be.
A climb to the top of a slender birch,
Riding it down to earth again,
Will have to do.

KNITTING

by Phyllis Hutchins

Knitting is comforting contentment. Knitting just feels good. In fact, it is a privilege for me. I am somewhat restricted by osteoporosis.

Restricted or not, when I knit, I feel that I accomplished something worthwhile. I remember, with great fondness, three old neighbors, sisters who could recall the late 1800's. They would watch TV only if they were knitting. Otherwise, they explained, they would be wasting their time.

I didn't learn to knit until my children were nearly grown. When I was a child, my mother didn't have time to knit. She made our mittens by sewing two pieces of knitted or woven material together in the form of a mitten. She trimmed it, turned it inside out, and bound the cuffs. Some people still do that, and it works as well now as it did then. It also works for scarves and pot holder mitts.

I knit for my grandchildren. It's lucky that I did. One little character lost a mitten. He usually wore a mismatched set.

My grandchildren are grown now. As older ladies knit for my children years ago, I now knit for others. There are many others. I donate my knitting to RSVP to be sold at the Aroostook Area Agency on Aging fall craft fair. They need mittens, hats, scarves, slippers, socks, and what-have-you. A friend knits for boxes given by her church to those who can best use the items. Another friend knits and crochets afghans and slippers for wheelchair-bound friends. Elementary school teachers and food kitchen helpers know who needs something. Also, knitting adds a personal touch to presents for family and friends.

We in northern Maine have a variety of yarn available. Most United States yarn is acrylic. It knits into good items, and is best for those allergic to wool. My favorite, Canadian wool yarn is available not far away. 100% wool yarn wears well and makes warm items. However, a clothes dryer will shrink it several sizes. I like 20% nylon and 80% wool yarn. It is as warm as all-wool yarn but is softer and washes better. In recent years, cotton yarn, which knits into good dish clothes, has been available.

Be aware that wool yarn is irritating to some people. Wearing a thin layer of nylon under the wool sometimes helps. Also, it can be just too darn hot. A friend double knit her husband a pair of socks, and he couldn't wear them because they were too hot.

Knitting isn't expensive. A few dollars will buy several sizes of needles, yarn, and instruction booklets. For about five dollars worth of yarn, I knit a hat and three pairs of children's mittens.

I don't consider myself good at knitting, but I have more than enough to do. I do, however, admire the fine knit and crochet work some of my friends do. Perhaps making new friends through knitting is as important as knitting itself.

Knitting is not a dying art. A recent newspaper article explained that many young women, twenty- to forty-years old, are learning to knit. Good for them.

The Tale of the Troubled Tree
by Rachel Burden

Introduction: This small tale evolved from many hours spent at my dining room table, keeping an eye on all the doings on Allen Street, after my devotions and crossword puzzle were finished. My grafted apple tree was foremost in my vision and with all the seasonal changes, it seemed to be telling me a story. True or not, at least it was fun to do and a great way to forget dusting!

Who would ever guess that my story would get into print! Look at me! I'm that scrawny, bent apple tree that you walk by on your way to school. I seldom rate attention unless the occasional passer-by gazes with pity or derision. Even the youngsters have given up trying to steal an apple on the sly. Old age has stolen my virility and my charm, but there were better days and my memory entertains me, snatching me back about fifty years. Then I felt useful and needed.

Roots are important and I have good ones. Somewhere, someone recognized that the little natural fruit apple tree might be a prime candidate for grafting. My adopted brothers were MacIntosh, Baldwin and Cortland and united we were a productive family. I tried to imitate my big brothers so intently, that soon I couldn't tell my looks from theirs and I loved them all equally.

When I sent blossoms that first spring, each grafted part took turns flowering, lasting longer than my neighbor, the flowering crab tree. I loved the deep pink of his artistry, but our several shades of pink and white really did glorify the neighborhood a few days longer. The birds and bees found me, singing, darting and pollinating. What fun, as I watched my family of apples develop, slowly. The human family enjoyed fresh fruit, applesauce, jelly and pies. Children climbed up through my branches. Birds flew in early and stayed late. Oh, I felt so useful and important!

Gradually troubles seemed to find me. First it was the worms. The humans checked with an orchard expert to find out how to spray. The directions said that it must be done three times. The first when the leaves are the size of a mouse's ear, the second when the buds show color and then ten days later. Back to the expert to find out why that didn't work. Oh, you must spray the flowering crab also or your diligence in fighting worms is useless. It seemed that every year my beautiful apples increased in size and volume. It seemed every year I watched the waste as they fell and rotted. What good was I? Why doesn't someone cut me down?!

Yet more adventures were to come. The human teenage boy while learning to control gears in the family truck, tried reverse when he meant forward and I felt a mighty impact. The accident left me crippled and I was sure the end was near, but it seemed that they wanted to give me another chance for life. I cooperated by doing lots of straining and bending until all were amazed to see how well my body had recovered. Did I really deserve this reprieve?

The years sped by. Beautiful blossoms pleased family and neighbors, rosy red apples trimmed me like a special Christmas tree, birds nibbled at the fruit (or was it for the worms?) and then the inevitable waste as my babies lay beneath me rotting away until the first snow blanket hid their ugliness.

Now for the worst of all in this little history. Vicious winds assaulted me one fall and winter, three of them. The first was the worst and I lost half of me—my better half. Now surely my sadness and deformity will prompt the human family to cut me down and let me have a peaceful death. I'm not useful in life anymore. NO, I hear. The spring blossoms are so beautiful. The tree must live! What would the birds think? There are still twelve apples on me and here comes a flock of grosbeaks who look so hungry. I think I can wait a little longer, but then a second BIG wind torments me and as I scan the damage, I count eleven apples on the ground. Little last apple, how did you escape that fearful storm? Did you feel that I needed your strength and comfort? You certainly can never weather another storm like that. The third wind came. The house people had windows shaking and the yard light ruined.

If you travel up Allen Street, take note of a tired, crippled apple tree with one battered red apple still clinging to a top branch. I'm so proud of his courage. Maybe I'll hang on a little bit longer.

The original format of this story is graced with photos of the little apple tree as it grew over the years.

BIATHLON
by Leonard Hutchins

Biathlon! Right here in northern Maine. My dream came true.

High school sports programs were suspended during World War II. When competition resumed in 1946, I learned that I was too awkward for basketball. However, my mother taught me as a child to snowshoe. It took a while, but I also learned to ski cross-country. I learned skiing down a hill, too, once. At least, I made the Fort Fairfield High School winter sports team.

Hunting and rifle shooting were part of my life. On a day off from school, I tied a clothesline-rope sling on my .22 rifle and tried hunting on skis. It didn't work. Maneuvering skis in a thick, bushy rabbit swamp was impossible. However, skiing to and from the swamp was great. Skis and rifles, for whatever reason, went together.

Soon after the war, Olympic competition also resumed, and I acquired a dream. From newsreels, I learned that other people, mostly from the Scandinavian countries, also realized that skis and rifles went together. The sport was called biathlon, and it seemed to me like the thing to do. But there was no biathlon in northern Maine.

Later, at the University of Maine there were Reserve Officer Training Corps and college rifle teams on which to shoot. Married and less than a gifted student, I had no time for ski team, and there was no biathlon team. Later still, during the years spent in the army and army reserve there was no biathlon team. Also, athletic competition wise, I was getting on in years.

During those years, national television stations provided far better than newsreel coverage of Olympic Games. At those times, my age notwithstanding, I revisited my dream of biathlon competition. I wondered, "Could I have made it?"

A few years ago on our local television station, plans for biathlon facilities were discussed. Here! In northern Maine! It seems that we have snow when other places do not. We always knew that, and, finally, Olympic organizers found out.

Still, planning and talking about such a great opportunity is one thing. Achieving such a program is something else. I hoped for the best. At seventy-something, I realized that I would not be a biathlon competitor. I hoped for the best for youngsters who might share my dream.

It happened. The facilities were built. The program was put in place. Biathlon competition arrived in northern Maine. Both national and international events now happen here.

Best of all, some of our youngsters share my dream. They have great facilities and coaches, and local volunteers to help run the events. Already, one of our young ladies can compete at international level. Who says dreams don't come true?

If you volunteer at a biathlon event, please wish the youngsters well for me. They are living my dream.

January, 2003

The Authors and Friends
Rachel Burden

Rachel Burden was born in 1921. Her parents were Ray and Hazel Higgins of Mapleton. She married Fred Burden in 1948. He served as school principal for Mapleton, Calais, and Caribou schools. Together they raised three children, Cheryl, Kathryn and Stephen (teachers  all) and have 5 grandchildren (two of whom are published, ordained pastors) and 12 great-grandchildren.

Rachel loved teaching. Her educational journey led her from Mapleton High School, to three years at UMPI (Aroostook State Normal School) and one year at Gorham for a BS. Because of the Depression and WWII, finances were difficult and an education was precious. She taught for 26 ½ years, mostly elementary grades. One of the most satisfying parts of teaching was encouraging young people to write and then sharing their sense of pride and joy.

She has written five family biographies, two of which are published. Now in happy retirement she still loves writing!

William McConnell

William McConnell was born in 1916 and has been a participant in wilderness adventures his entire life. Had he time to write while living through various phases in the woods, he might have challenged Henry  David Thoreau for an understanding of what living close to nature is truly about. It was a tough life when, as the oldest child of six, he followed his father's boot-steps into the wilderness to eke out a living during the Great Depression. Although he never felt temperamentally or physically suited to the life he found himself in, he did his share in support of his family.

Through his indelible memory, Bill wrote about his early years in the fact-filled book, *Notes from the Packbasket,* and continues to write essays about the days when, if you wanted to eat, you worked—often before sunup and after sundown. Somehow through it all, Bill manages to recall the joys of childhood and teen years where he was happiest sitting in the sunshine with his nose in a book.

Maxine Smith

Maxine Smith is a farmer's daughter who married a farmer's son, Vaughn Smith, in 1943. Together they raised three children, Sandra, Scott, and Randy, while farming in Mapleton, Maine. Maxine attended Presque Isle Schools and graduated from Aroostook State

Normal School (UMPI) in 1942, and went on for a Master's degree in Remedial Reading Supervision from UMO in 1970. She taught school for many years while Vaughn farmed and worked as a pilot on daily trips to Boston and back for George Higgins Flying Service to supplement their farm income.

For Maxine, writing has been a way to preserve family history and an outlet for the expression of love she holds for family and friends. Some of Maxine's essays take the form of grace-filled poetry. In her words to her granddaughter:

When heartstrings join our lives for such a short, sweet, while;
    And happy memories are born; a long, long line of love is drawn
To tie you close even when you're far away. That line is strong,
    And you will always know that you can follow it and hang on tight.

Maxine and Vaughn, now married 73 years, reside at Leisure Village.

Leonard Hutchins was born in Fort Fairfield in 1930 and was lucky enough to convince Phyllis Schwartz to marry him in 1950. He earned  both bachelor's and master's degrees from the University of Maine, served in the military and taught school in Hampden and Ashland. In 1968 these two dreamers purchased and restored the Oxbow Lodge where they fed and entertained hundreds of hungry folk from around the state and housed hundreds of sportsmen from all over the United States during the magnificent hunting seasons for which the Oxbow area is famous. All this, while raising four well-rounded, indulgent children.

Over the years Leonard listened to students, relatives, neighbors and guests, gathering folklore to write about later on. Together with Phyllis they produced a cookbook, and a book of short stories, *Gram, Is He Telling Me the Truth?* More recently he published a fictionalized version of life in a North Maine Woods lumber camp during the early 20th century called *BonHomme*.

His extensive essays have been published in *Maine Life, Maine Sportsman, The Rolling Log* and *Echoes*. A recent work, *I Love to Fly*, written during the months before his wife's death in October, 2015, involves Santa Claus, reindeer, and a young girl who learns the "scientific" reason for Santa's ability to fly. This delightful book is in search of an illustrator.

Marilyn Chase

Marilyn Chase was born in Fort Fairfield, Maine on October 23, 1929, the daughter of Carleton and Grace Whiteneck Hoyt. She graduated from the much-loved Maple Grove Grammar School and Fort Farifield High School (1947), University of Maine, Orono (1951) with a BA in Theater and Journalism, and a M.Ed., UMPG (1974). From 1950 to 1970 she was married to the late Richard W. Sprague, the father of her children: Jonathan, Christopher, Susan, and Robin.

She worked for several newspapers as a feature writer and later taught English, speech and drama at Houlton High School. After marrying Philip S. Chase Jr. in 1970, she worked as a speech and language therapist in Brunswick.

In 1988 they moved back to the Hoyt homestead farm in Fort Fairfield where she continued speech and language therapy in the Easton Public Schools for 10 years.

Donna Pelletier

Donna Pelletier loves to cook—everything from muffins, home-baked beans, banana bread, cookies and more and she is generous with her goodies. "Bring me some of your apples, Martie, and I'll make us all a nice big apple crisp."

It is not surprising that this photograph captures Donna, in the hat, and her best friend Marilyn Chase giggling like schoolgirls. When together, there is a part of them that just flows backward in time to their days at Maple Grove Elementary School in Fort Fairfield. Donna writes of a teacher sending the two off to fetch his lunch from a home over the hill nearly every day. Donna seems to think it was because they were so trustworthy. Perhaps the man just needed a break.

Unfortunately, recent health challenges have kept Donna from regular attendance at our twice-weekly writing group meetings, but when she is with us she just lights up the room. She and Marilyn often have the group in stitches, although we don't always know why. What we do know is that Donna is the keeper of a myriad of delightful memories of growing-up years in Fort Fairfield, Maine. It is our hope that she'll soon be back with us writing up a storm with wit and wisdom fine-tuned over decades.

Marjorie Bishop

Marjorie Bishop has lived her entire life in Presque Isle. She was born in the Sweetser-Connick Hospital on Highland Avenue (now Dudley Street). She was one of the first three babies delivered by Dr. Storer Boone at the beginning of his practice. Her family continued

with him until, after many years, he ended his practice. She attended local schools, and the University of Maine. She taught a total of 31 years.

Her parents were T. Earle and Lela (Mooers) Everett. She had three younger brothers, Eugene, Howard, and Ronald. She was to married Dana H. Bishop "for 63 years filled with fun and laughter." They had one daughter, Marcia, who married David J. Fletcher—they both graduated from Tufts University and both got advanced degrees at U of M, she in library science and he in law. Marjorie has two grandchildren—Emily, a graduate of Brown University and Bill, who graduated from

Wheaton. Emily married Andrew Murphy and brought her three step-great-grandchildren, Andrew, Shawn, and Kylie, then another great-granddaughter, Mackenzie Dana. Bill married Sue Unger-Leiter and added three more great-grandchildren—Alexis and twins, Delaney and Harrison. Marjorie, a proud great-grandmother, describes her newest generation as "Loving, Caring, Precious, Super! " and adds, "How can one be so Lucky?"

Joan Allen

Joan Allen has been absorbed by genealogy research for many years. She married Vaughn Allen and together they raised three children, William, Joel and Vaughn. Her stories reflect sharp memories of a happy childhood in Presque Isle, the only child of Otis and Alta Nichols Stevens, born in 1927.

Joan spent hours at the Presque Isle Library with her mother, who loved books. It was natural for her to develop her own love of reading early. She was a favorite of the librarian who would pick out books, like *Bambi*, that she thought this precocious child should read.

Working for Arthur C. Perry Insurance Company on Maine Street, Joan's dad was always ready to drop everything when he saw his daughter walking down the steep hill on State Street toward his shop. The shop was situated between a druggist and a jewelry store. After a big hug, the two would enter the jewelry store so together they could admire all the beautiful things. Next, the two would head for the drug store and the certain joy of an ice cream for both—always chocolate, of course.

Her dad walked home for lunch every day, all the way up State Street. He never owned a car but his brother, Fred P. Stevens, owner of the men's clothing store on Maine Street, often took the family for a drive.

Of all her memories, the favorite is of her beloved cousins, three Graves children and two Reynolds children, who would often join her at Nanny's house for hours of play. She always hoped to be invited to their homes for dinner because it was more fun than eating in her quiet home on Summit Street.

Norma Ouellette

Norma Ouellette was born in Caribou, Maine, August 16, 1931, the daughter of Tom and Cora Raymond Cyr. In 1949 she married Roger Ouellette and together they traveled the world with their four children, Steven, Anne, Julie, and Alan.

Fascinated by airplanes, for a while Norma thought only of being a stewardess for a big airline. Instead she shared her husband Roger's love of flight as he served in the armed forces in Vietnam flying small fixed-wing crafts and helicopters.

She loves music, played piano in her heyday and loved to dance. She enjoys an extensive collection of giraffe figurines and room décor.

Although now functionally blind, she writes of her great adventures with clarity and a unique voice reflecting the joy she feels in life. The residents who eat lunch together in the Leisure Village dining room look forward to Norma's daily offering of an appetizer in the form of delicious fresh-pealed slices of cucumbers. They wonder how she grows them during the cold winter months. (We'll keep her secret of the grocery delivery.)

Joyce Davis

Joyce Davis was born May 4, 1927, the daughter of Elmer and Ottobelle Worthen Spencer. She was raised by her grandparents Frank and Anna Lunny Worthen and later by her Aunt Rona and Uncle Lou.

Graduating from high school near the end of WWII she received her nurse training in the final graduating class in the Army Nurse Corps. She married Arnie Davis and together they raised three children: Susan, Bob, and Steve.

As an oncology nurse for 40 years, she retired from The Aroostook Medical Center, Presque Isle. Joyce is an inspiration for many, but none so much as her son Steve who retired from engineering in the Midwest and came home to study nursing. He is now a nurse at TAMC like his mom.

Leila Day

Leila Day retired from many years as a telephone operator. She witnessed first-hand the conversion from the old plug-and-talk phone system to computer assisted telephone service. While working full time

for the telephone company she helped her father raise her two youngest sisters. Leila remains close with her sister Charlene who lives in Presque Isle.

Leila attends Bible study faithfully and does not take her good health for granted. She is serious about physical activity as she had heart bypass surgery while still working for the telephone company.

Though not a prolific writer, Leila is a faithful member of the Leisure Village Writers and often contributes her unique perspective to discussions. Leila is generally an early arrival and is always ready to lend a hand whenever she sees another member trying to find a seat.

Roger Oakes

Roger Oakes is one of the Leisure Village Writers' founding members, involved since the spring of 2015. He faithfully attends our twice weekly get-togethers and is occasionally joined by his wife Geraldine. A gentle man, it is easy to imagine him leading a group of Boy Scouts on great adventures in the 1960s. St. Mary's Catholic Church was their den but the State of Maine their laboratory in the study of and preparation for life.

Roger is a sunny optimist. Though he enjoys the luxury of "sleeping-in" he doesn't complain about interrupting his rest to make his way to the writing group. As a matter of fact, Roger never has a negative word to say about anything. No matter how many people are gathered around after our meeting, Roger always waits to make eye-contact and say, "Thank you. I really enjoyed that." His courtesy is appreciated!

He and his wife Geraldine reside together at Leisure Village and together still attend weekly Mass at St. Mary's Catholic Church.

OTHER PARTICIPANTS

Where would story-tellers be without an audience? Leisure Village Writers are fortunate to have several story-lovers who join our meetings regularly. It is always so much fun to read to our attentive friends. Thanks Ladies for being part of our group! We hope soon to help you write some of your stories.

Rolinda (Lindy) Fowler

Patty Bell

Gloria Sandstrom

It was not easy to locate as many photos as we wanted to include. Over the years many retirees have downsized, passing family photos on to next generations.

Childhood divider photos are all from Rachel Higgins Burden's family photo album. The large centered photo with the dog shows a small, worried-looking Rachel positioned far away from the scary beast. The small centered photo has Irwin, Rachel, and Mariam lined up waiting for the school team. Studio photos are of Rachel and her brother, Irwin Higgins.

Adult divider photo is the studio portrait of the three young Higgins adults. An interesting note to this is that the family couldn't afford individual senior pictures at that time, so they compromised. Irwin was in his second year of college, Rachel (seated) was the high school senior, and Mariam would be a high school senior the following year.

Married Life divider shows Joyce and Arnie Davis in a photo taken of framed snapshots in Joyce's apartment. Photographs were a luxury back when they married. The oval is a photo of an original pencil drawing by Roger Ouellette given to his wife, Norma. At about two feet tall in an oak frame it holds a place of honor in Norma's apartment. A close up view shows the inscription on the rings.

New Generations divider shows a large Hutchins family reunion. At left bottom, Marjorie Bishop with her father, T. Earle Bishop, holding Marjorie's daughter Marcia Bishop; with her grandfather, Everett Bishop, at the left. The photo on the right has Rachel's Grandmother Higgins holding a grandchild (Rachel's sister Barbara) and a great-grandchild surrounded by other great-grandchildren.

Way Back When divider photos are from the Higgins family album. The car is the Model T she writes about. The top photo is Rachel and Mariam with mother Hazel Higgins. Bottom left shows Ray Higgins as he changes one of his hundreds of flats. Right bottom finds Rachel and Irwin Higgins ready to play in the snow with a toy fashioned from a potato barrel.

Golden Years divider shows a large gathering of Leisure Village Writers and friends. Below left, Phyllis Hutchins with a new great-grandbaby; top right, Joyce and Arnie Davis boating; and bottom right, the Hutchins family gathered with canine friends: back row—Paul, Leonard, Susan, and Peter; seated—Phyllis and Dorothy.

ACKNOWLEDGEMENTS

The Leisure Village Writers would like to thank the following publications for their support over the years as, piece by piece, our efforts have been accepted for inclusion in the fine work they contribute to our community.

Echoes: The Northern Maine Journal of Rural Culture

The Star-Herald Newspaper, Presque Isle, Maine

Fort Fairfield: It's Time to Tell Our Stories, 1858-2008,
Rayle Reed Ainsworth and Sarah Ulman

The following are directly quoted with permission of the authors:

Tater Picking Scientist: Selected Writings of Irwin R. Higgins
Compiled by Rachel Higgins Burden, 1999

Ray Higgins: His Mapleton Memories,
by Rachel Higgins Burden, 1981

Notes From The Packbasket, by William McConnell

The unpublished collected works of Maxine Lovely Smith

Our thanks go to the following for inspiration:

SAGE: Seniors Achieving Greater Education,
University of Maine: Presque Isle

Wiser Living: Living Wiser After 50

People Plus News: The Center that Builds Community

Speaking Frankly by Frank D. Connors

The Presque Isle Historical Society

Aroostook Area Agency on Aging

Mark and Emily Turner Memorial Library, Presque Isle, Maine

Thanks to the Top of the Lake Snowmobile Museum, in Naubinway, Michigan for permission to use the story and photo of the Model T snowmobile. Imagine, reaching all the way to Michigan to learn more about northern Maine history!

Thanks also to the James School, the one room schoolhouse on the Niles Road in Presque Isle, for the use of the photo of the old school team.

Thanks and much love to Kathleen Dampf for her great job interviewing a member of our group for this publication. (See cover photo.)

This book would not have been possible without the support of our Number One Fan: Tina Ruest, Activity Director for Leisure Gardens Inc.

Tina not only makes it possible for us to meet twice a week at "The Village," but she takes time from her personal world to show up whenever we need her.

Thanks also to the good people at Leisure Village and Leisure Gardens especially Albert Cyr, Greg Cyr, and Doug Cyr for graciously welcoming our friend, Martie Pritchard, into our sphere.

Martie's deepest gratitude goes to Marina Kirsch, her pilot, her guide, her mentor, and her friend, who confidently began this publishing journey with her and has kept her going when she felt like throwing her hands up. Intending to write a book, publishing a book, and producing a quality work are all different aspects of the process. Marina provided editing, cover and interior design, and assistance in publishing. "A book is only *good* when it's done," she said. "But don't rush it—when it's done, you will *know* it's done!" A quest for perfection is the touchstone of her character and she has enabled us to produce this important work while teaching the fine points of writing and publishing.

About Martha Brabant Pritchard

Martha Brabant Pritchard, Martie, lives with husband Jim on an old dairy farm in Chapman, Maine. For twenty-two years the two have worked to save the century-old, post and beam, three-story barn which is central to their 200-acre farm—The Barking Barn Farm. Though not farmers by any stretch of the imagination, they keep a flock of chickens, geese, ducks, and a single turkey. Several animal-shelter rescue-rabbits enjoy large cages within the "chicken room." Two mules, an appaloosa horse, and two mini horses round out the barn population. In the past, goats, pigs, and sheep graced the hallowed halls of the barn. Neighbor kids kept an assortment of horses, ponies, and cows as well. Always looking for a good use of the farmland, the rich, abandoned acres jump-started "Farm for ME" a Catholic Charities venture that now provides thousands of pounds of locally raised, fresh and frozen produce for Aroostook County food pantries.

Jim and Martie's four children have given them the gift of eleven grandchildren and a new great-granddaughter. Never without animals in their lives, three cats and four dogs are presently in residence in their old farmstead. A golden retriever, Bright Star, posed for the logo for this book and future publications.

Throughout her life, Martie has been open to new experiences and opportunities. She says she was an accidental teacher. She explains, "I didn't want to be a teacher because I had such terrible experiences in school. When I ruled out nursing (blood), secretary (typing), airline pilot (in the 70s?) and veterinarian (Cornell just laughed when they discovered that Martie was a girl), I settled for teaching."

But she'd promised herself that she would be not be just a *good* teacher. She'd be a *great* teacher and would leave teaching before she became stale. For that reason, she purposely varied her career through all levels of elementary education, then seventh grade life science, and finally third through fifth grade self-contained special education. She found the last assignment to be the most rewarding of all, but also the most challenging. Managing a classroom that grew from seven handicapped students to sixteen; she wore herself out and was blessed with a wake-up call in the form of a minor heart attack at age fifty-nine.

She retired and aimed her sights at writing. In eight years she completed a not-yet-published biography, *From Bombs to Babies*, which is what she was doing when she found herself inspired to write this book with the Leisure Village Writers.

She earned a BS from Mansfield State College, and an MS in Reading Supervision from University of Scranton, both in Pennsylvania. In 1996 she was named Outstanding Middle Level Educator by the Maine Association for Middle Level Education (MAMLE).

Martie is well prepared for the new path her career is taking, convinced that history is held in trust in the hearts and minds of community elders. She is actively seeking book presentations, signings, interviews, and lectures or seminars to encourage others to become involved with seniors in their own towns and cities.

As a Leisure Village Writer put it, "Martie opened a window for me."

It only takes a little effort to "open windows," find hidden treasures, and record them for future generations.

How to reach Martie:

Email: martie.farm@gmail.com or martiewrites@yahoo.com

On Facebook: Author Martha Pritchard

Website: MarthaPritchard.com

Old-fashioned telephone: 207-764-1620

Suggestions on How to Use this Book

This anthology is not an ordinary work of nonfiction. Written by thirteen separate voices it represents a variety of perspectives covering nine decades of first-hand experiences as well as a few glimpses back even farther.

The book is loosely organized into six categories of memories. This offers the reader many options for experiencing the stories. Above all, do not feel bound to reading the book from page one to the end. I suggest opening the book at random. Leaf through and find a story title that tickles your curiosity and begin. When you discover an author that speaks to you in a certain way, why not turn to the table of contents and find another piece by the same author and continue with that "conversation."

You'll discover a variety of language mechanics that are different from the way we write today. Check out what some editors might call "errors," and discover different traditions in English grammar that have evolved over the decades. You'll learn that the English language is a moving, growing body of rules which fit a changing society. It will remain so, as long as we don't pay too much attention to the word-processor-genies and continue to write with creativity and in our own style.

Perhaps you are interested in railroads. Scan the table of contents and travel the rails our writers have known. Cooking? There are even a few recipes sprinkled within the stories. Find what interests you and follow your own path through this book. Then return to the pieces you missed and be open to surprises.

Don't forget bedtime stories. Children who have grown beyond fairy tales and talking animal stories are ready for nonfiction. Many of these stories can fill that need and will undoubtedly spark interest in connected history. Communicate with your child's teacher or school librarian when such an interest is piqued, and he or she may be able to use that new interest as a home-to-school connection. A child might enjoy writing a letter to one of our writers. Our writers would treasure such communication, no matter how brief. Address? Use the author's name, Leisure Village, Presque Isle, ME 04769. The Post Office will do the rest.

A Message to Elders and Volunteers

We all have experiences worth preserving, and what was accomplished by the Leisure Village Writers, can be achieved by senior groups anywhere. Will children in 2025 know what life was like when the family telephone was connected to a wire that ran out a hole in the wall to a pole outside the house? Will they know what it was like to pay for groceries with cash instead of plastic? Will they know that a set of books, called an encyclopedia, used to be found in many homes, schools, and libraries, and that these books were often the first source of information that people turned to?

By gathering together with others interested in writing and sharing stories, seniors can ignite imagination and memories and encourage each other to write. In the Leisure Village group, one participant talked about tobogganing in her youth. She was encouraged to "write it down," and that story led to another memory, and then another. As a result of a single memory and much encouragement from the group, a previously reluctant author produced three separate stories.

Retirees and high school students are ideal volunteers to help seniors begin gathering stories and photographs at assisted living facilities, retirement communities, senior centers, and nursing homes. By contacting the activities director, showing a copy of this book, and offering assistance to start a writers' group, a volunteer can create an opportunity for intellectual stimulation for residents and preservation of local history and culture that might otherwise be lost to posterity.

To paraphrase one of our writers, "all it takes is opening a window to discover how much history is waiting for a breeze to ignite the memories of an elder."

Martha Brabant Pritchard is available for workshops, lectures, or consultations to help jump-start the formation of writer's groups in other areas. How to reach her:

By email: martie.farm@gmail.com
Via her website: MarthaPritchard.com
Via old-fashioned telephone: 207-764-1620

78197086R00144